UNFUCK YOUR ADDICTION

Using Science to Free Yourself from Harmful Reliance on Substances, Habits, and Out of Control Behaviors

Dr. Faith G. Harper, LPC-S, ACS, ACN

Microcosm Publishing
Portland, Ore | Cleveland, Ohio

UNFUCK YOUR ADDICTION: Using Science to Free Yourself from Harmful Reliance on Substances, Habits, and Out of Control Behaviors

© Dr. Faith G. Harper, 2023

First edition - 5,000 copies - July 18, 2023
ISBN 978-1-62106-283-7
This is Microcosm #349
Edited by Lex Orgera
Cover and design by Joe Biel
This edition © Microcosm Publishing, 2023
For a catalog, write or visit:
Microcosm Publishing
2752 N Williams Ave.
Portland, OR 97227

www.Microcosm.Pub/Addiction

To join the ranks of high-class stores that feature Microcosm titles, talk to your rep: In the U.S. **COMO** (Atlantic), **ABRAHAM** (Midwest), **BOB BARNETT** (Texas, Oklahoma, Louisiana), **IMPRINT** (Pacific), **TURNAROUND** (Europe), **UTP/ MANDA** (Canada), **NEW SOUTH** (Australia/New Zealand), **GPS** in Asia, Africa, India, South America, other countries, or **FAIRE** and **EMERALD** in the gift trade.

Did you know that you can buy our books directly from us at sliding scale rates? Support a small, independent publisher and pay less than Amazon's price at **www.Microcosm.Pub**

Global labor conditions are bad, and our roots in industrial Cleveland in the '70s and '80s made us appreciate the need to treat workers right. Therefore, our books are MADE IN THE USA.

Library of Congress Cataloging-in-Publication Data

Names: Harper, Faith G., author.
Title: Unfuck your addiction : using science to free yourself from harmful
  reliance on substances, habits, and out of control behaviors / by Faith
  G. Harper, PhD, LPC-S, ACS, ACN.
Description: Portland, OR : Microcosm Publishing, [2022] | Summary: "We
  have almost all been addicted to something at some point, or had a habit
  spiral out of control. But what does that mean? What exactly are
  addictions and out of control behaviors, why do we get caught up in
  them, and how do we get our lives back? Bestselling author Dr. Faith
  Harper and addictions counselor Joe Green join forces to help those of
  us struggling (or supporting others) with problematic use of alcohol,
  drugs, gambling, work, food, sex, shopping, screens, gaming, self-harm,
  or anything else where we've crossed a line. Their perspective is down
  to earth, realistic, and refreshing. You'll learn about the brain
  science behind addiction, how to tell if something is a problem or about
  to become one, how to find your way out of unhealthy behaviors, and how
  to avoid passing them down to the next generation. No matter what paths
  you've taken in life, you can absolutely learn to fulfill your needs in
  ways that are healthy for yourself and the people around you"-- Provided
  by publisher.
Identifiers: LCCN 2022014625 | ISBN 9781621062837 (trade paperback)
Subjects: LCSH: Compulsive behavior. | Compulsive behavior--Treatment.
Classification: LCC RC533 .H366 2022 | DDC 616.85/84--dc23/eng/20220629
LC record available at https://lccn.loc.gov/2022014625

Microcosm Publishing is Portland's most diversified publishing house and distributor, with a focus on the colorful, authentic, and empowering. Our books and zines have put your power in your hands since 1996, equipping readers to make positive changes in their lives and in the world around them. Microcosm emphasizes skill-building, showing hidden histories, and fostering creativity through challenging conventional publishing wisdom with books and bookettes about DIY skills, food, bicycling, gender, self-care, and social justice. What was once a distro and record label started by Joe Biel in a drafty bedroom was determined to be *Publishers Weekly*'s fastest-growing publisher of 2022 and #3 in 2023, now among the oldest independent publishing houses in Portland, OR, and Cleveland, OH. We are a politically moderate, centrist publisher in a world that has inched to the right for the past 80 years.

TABLE OF CONTENTS

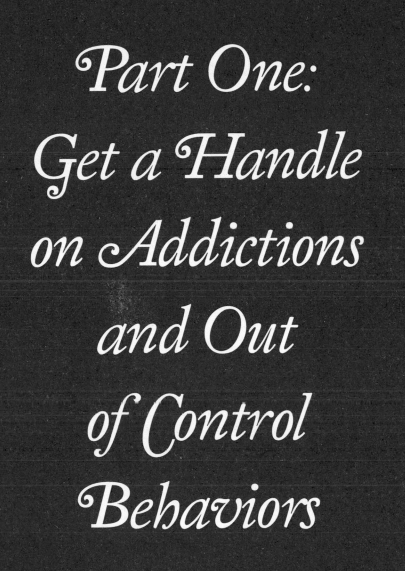

Part One: Get a Handle on Addictions and Out of Control Behaviors

INTRODUCTION

I feel like a middle-aged crank, quite likely because I am one, but in this case, especially with this particular book, my crankiness turned out to be important. Because while there is a ton of misinformation and disinformation out there around mental health issues, it is especially difficult to parse out how to approach and seek treatment for both addictions and out of control behaviors. It shouldn't be this hard. And the fact that it is, indeed, this hard is giving me gray hairs and RBF. So many people are desperate for answers. Or at least a decent starting point in finding them.

We are talking about issues that we collectively recoil from on the regular. Because of stigma and shame. Guilt and embarrassment. We are overwhelmed and under supported. To most of the people around us, we are not allowed to be anything other than "fine."

This book is intended to spark a new conversation. To get granular about what the science really says (at least as of this writing) about what constitutes an addiction and what is categorized as problematic or out of control behavior. To invite a different openness to our struggles. We are, most of us, anything but fine. We're exhausted and scared and lonely and secretly (or maybe even not-so-secretly) worried that we are unsalvageable human beings not deserving of care.

If you were in my office right now, I would make you a mug of tea. Sit across from you while you drink it. And repeat as often as it takes for you to believe me that you are so deserving of care. You don't need to be salvaged because you are not broken. You are having a normal reaction to an abnormal world. You were searching for ways to cope, which worked until the coping skill became a bigger problem than the original problem. You may be scared and hurting and feeling alone. You may feel like you really fucked things up. But if you are reading this book now? Even with deep and eye-rolly suspicion? You are showing a glimmer of hope.

And that's all we need to start you on the path to recovery.

WHAT *IS* AN ADDICTION ANYWAY?

The World Before Addiction Was Addiction: A Historical Perspective

This section is important. Not because I am a ranty crank (we already established that) but because it helps us truly see the problem (or lack thereof) over time. And how modern solutions morphed into more horrific problems. It also shows why treatment is so hard to access and why so many people are such astonishing assholes to those who are struggling. Modern culture created the problem that is now punishing rather than solving.

One of the most interesting books I've read on this topic is by Antonio Escohotado. It's the only book of his translated into English, and it's called *A Brief History of Drugs: From the Stone Age to the Stoned Age.* Escohotado was a lawyer from a well-off, intellectual family in Spain. Because of his research regarding community and legal responses to drug use, he is often referred to as a libertarian.[1] In reality, he was a

---

1 When someone is referred to as having libertarian ideals or termed a conspiracy theorist, I automatically become really interested in what they are saying that upsets people so much. Sometimes it

philosopher and socialist who was calling bullshit on racist, misogynistic, religious, xenophobic, aporophobic systems across Western, industrialized culture.

Escohotado points out that drugs have existed throughout human history. Quite literally. He begins with using the Hippocratic[2] definition of a drug as something that overcomes the body rather than something the body overcomes. Food is something the body overcomes, right? It breaks down and is converted into energy. Drugs are things that overcome the body, and generally in much smaller doses than food because they alter our state of being in some way. Seeds from psychoactive plants have been found at sites where humans lived as far back as the seventh millennium BCE. The use of drugs themselves have been depicted in art and writing as far back as the tenth century BCE. Drugs are so intertwined with human development that many scientists think it likely that drug use (especially psychedelics) is responsible for many of the evolutionary advances made to the human body, especially our brains. Drugs provided energy, relieved pain, and assisted humans in their spiritual quests.

According to Escohotado, drugs (and alcohol) weren't the problem, but there were warnings across religious texts about the dangers of inebriation. The stance wasn't "don't use anything," it was "don't get messy about it . . . manage

---

is pretty batshit crazy. But other times, it is Antonio Escohotado handing the establishment their whole ass on a platter.
2 Hippocrates suggested opium for uterine pain. And, honestly? I'm not mad about it at all.

your shit." Most of the texts from these time periods refer to drunkenness as an occasional problem (to be dealt with by the family, not the state), and there was zero mention of opium abuse (as an example), even though it was being used by millions of people.

What changed? Christian sects started to take aim at drugs that overpower the body. They were signs of weakness. *If you are in pain, it's because God has declared it so. If you need a substance to get closer to God, you don't really love Him.* In fact, some sects taught that when Lucifer fell to the earth, he became the grapes we made into wine. Which meant wine was literally the work of the devil. Except priests were still allowed to drink it. Y'all? I couldn't make this shit up if I tried.

Paganism gave people (especially women) too much power. It allowed people to enjoy their bodies and enjoy sex. It encouraged management of pain and mitigation of suffering. All horrible ideas that must be eradicated, according to Christianity. The "discovery" of Turtle Island led to punishments of the people who already lived here for engaging in these practices. To this day, the remnants of how "witchcraft" was disparaged remain. Watch any movie or cartoon where witches are making potions . . . the use of frogs and toads still exists and is treated as if it is ridiculous and cruel. Guess what? Some toad skins contain DMT, which has significant analgesic effects when included in salves. Witches were pagan healers who didn't agree that people should endure pain and suffering for the sake of religious piety. And we can't have *that* perspective running around.

Around the same time that Christopher Columbus was running around pointing at shit that belonged to other people while yelling "that's MINE!" like a fucking toddler, the first European medical association was established in England, with the crown giving them exclusive rights to the treatment of British citizens. But they still had a problem with how to actually treat people as well as the "witches" did. And it wasn't just that European healers—who had been taught through local lineages and training—got legally excluded from their own healing methods. A good number of Spanish doctors traveled to Turtle Island to learn about the medical practices of all of these heathen-pagan-witchy practitioners and to steal whatever knowledge and substances they could.[3] The short story is that pagan drugs, sourced and provided by pagan treatment providers were co-opted by doctors, pharmacists, and chemists because it was decreed by governmental authorities that they were the only ones respectable enough to know about and use them.

Mind-altering medications still existed. You just weren't going to get them from a "witch." And as the industrial revolution took hold, there was increased need for pain medications (makes sense, right?). Opium, morphine, and heroin were commonly prescribed. Bayer packaged morphine and aspirin together in a double package, it was so common. Cocaine became available as a "bit of an upper." It was every-

---

3Ironically, they learned that the Aztecs maintained amazing medicinal gardens, and if you were poor you could show up there and receive treatment and medicine. Anyone. No money required. Too bad that idea didn't go back to Europe with them. Fuckers.

fucking-where. Coca leaves were in Coca-Cola. Freud was a huge fan of cocaine. In fact, he was paid in the product to make recommendations for it as a proto-influencer of the time.

So we continued on happily having access to drugs, though now they cost a lot more—until the 1900s. Remember that the United States was founded (colonized) by religious fundamentalists who thought only whores ever showed their ankles, right? Then they started bringing over all these more melanated people to build the shit they wanted to have in their new (stolen) country that became more and more melanated, and those people became harder and harder to control. It doesn't help that they were enslaved either literally or by circumstances. Also taking all their yummy drugs. And the racial wars around drugs began. Opium existed because the Chinese were bad. Cocaine was bad because it was used to extend an arduous work day by the descendents of the African diaspora (never mind that it was because they were drinking entirely-fucking-legal Coca-Cola), THC was the fault of the Mexicans, and alcohol was a problem of the Jews and the Irish. Good Christians don't do these things (remember that Irish Catholics were not considered Christian, they were idol worshippers, as much heathens as Jewish peoples). And the era of dry laws as a means of exerting racism flourished.

Certain drugs were still legally available. The amines (amphetamine and its party cousins) were popular through World War II in the US because they gave energy to soldiers and helped their depression. They also gave energy to their wives back home and kept those same wives skinny.[4]

So more and more synthetic isolates were made from plants, which led to more use and more problems. And more and more adulteration of these drugs. There are many rational arguments to be made that the deaths we see now are a result of these changes (Escohotado points out that there isn't any evidence of deaths related to even these stronger drugs before adulteration became an issue . . . and his work was completed in the nineties, before fentanyl was showing up in all kinds of drug supplies).

And what people were allowed to use and not use (and what punishments were levied if you were caught using) had deeply racist roots that we see in the system to this day. THC is now legal in many states, at least at some level of use. And more measures surrounding decriminalization are being debated at state and municipal levels. I'm writing this at a time where my city is looking to decriminalize THC and the state legislature is once again trying to decriminalize fentanyl test strips as a harm-reduction measure.

Decriminalization works, y'all. Go ahead and send me a yellcaps email about it if you think you need to, but in 2001, Portugal decriminalized all possession and personal use of

---

4 Another point to consider when people wring their hands about how fat Americans have gotten since this era. There are many reasons for our change in body mass over the past decades, which I've written about in my book *Unfuck Your Eating*, but also? Everyone would be hella skinny if we were popping dexies like they are M&M's, FFS.

literally every illicit drug (but will still come for you around trafficking and the like). They had a decrease in both drug-related deaths and new HIV infections. Decarceration of nonviolent offenders was something that happened in many larger cities (including my own) early during the Covid-19 outbreak, as well as adoption of "cite-and-release" programs for first-time, nonviolent offenses. And there was no related uptick in crime. In the US, we spend 750 times more money on legal action against people who use drugs than supporting and/or providing treatment services. And if we divest some of the funds away from drug law enforcement and use those funds to shore up harm reduction and treatment programs? What a fucking difference we could make.

Now, someone may want to play devil's advocate here and point out that there are still plenty of people who do not have an addiction. First of all? The devil doesn't need an advocate, and intellectual exercises waste time from providing people with actual help and care so I'm not super interested in such nonsense. But also? Sure. Even though there are far more people who are having issues with addiction than there used to be once drugs became industrialized, not everyone struggles with addiction. So what makes some people more likely than others to develop one?

Where Addictions Come From

Y'all? I wish I had a simple answer for you on this one. But there is no single variable that causes addiction. Very little in this world will affect all people the same way. Add in the fact that while some research focuses on abuse of and dependence on substances, much more research focuses on the etiology, or cause, of use. And use alone does not create an addiction, so we can't really map causes for use into causes of addiction, right?

That being said, I'm going to cover some of the factors that have been studied well enough that we can fairly confidently say at least contribute to addiction.

Biological Factors: This means both genetic and epigenetic vulnerability. Genetics refers to our actual genes and epigenetics is how those genes express (which are also heritable). Addictions do run in families. If a parent struggles with addiction, their biological children are three-to-four-times more vulnerable to addiction. Twins also have a high concordance rate, meaning if one twin struggles with addiction, chances are pretty decent that the other twin does too. But Doc, you're thinking, what if all of that is happening because their home life sucks, and it doesn't have to do with their genes? Good point, my smartie! That's where the adoption studies come in.

Individuals with biological parents with addiction issues have the same three-to-four-times higher risk of addiction even when raised by adoptive parents with no addiction issues.

Physiology, part of human biology, also seems to play a role, though it has been studied more with regards to alcoholism than other addictive substances. For example, individuals with the polymorphism of two particular liver enzymes have a biological protection against alcoholism. Aldehyde dehydrogenase (ALDH2) and alcohol dehydrogenase-2 (ADH2) are found more often in Asian individuals than in other ethnic groups, which may partially explain the lower rates of alcoholism among Asian folks.

Monoamine oxidase (MAO) is another biochemical marker that has been associated with alcoholism. MAO is an enzyme that impacts a multitude of brain neurotransmitters, including dopamine, norepinephrine, and serotonin, which all influence our behavior. Individuals who have an alcohol use disorder have significantly fewer MAO platelets.

Personality Traits: Certain personality traits have been tied to substance abuse, most notably antisocial behaviors, aggressive behaviors, and rebellious behaviors. This is (at least somewhat) different from biological factors. Some of our personality quirks are a result of genetics and / or epigenetics and some are traits we developed in response to other aspects of our lives, especially our early lives. If you grew up living in survival mode, for example, any of those just-mentioned personality traits may have been ones you developed to stay safe in fucked up situations. And if you had grown up having your needs generally met and felt loved and supported, you may have otherwise been a big ole softie of a human being.

And antisocial, aggressive, and rebellious behaviors are all anger-based protective personality dimensions. And what do substances do? They can either elevate those behaviors so you can really go off or they can soften them when you can't manage how shitty it feels to be so angry all the time.

Social Factors: Another huge catch-all category is social factors. The things that surround our lives, thus impacting them, are termed social learning. A multitude of social factors have been correlated with substance use disorders, including parental values around use, sibling values around use, peer values around use, lack of interest in academic achievement, the glorification of substances through media, growing up poor, growing up in unsafe communities, and social deprivation/isolation. So while personality traits are about both our genetics and our surrounding society, this is just society. And we may not be aggressive and rebellious people, but could still be in a situation where no one gives a fuck about our lives so why not go party? That's a social factor decision.

Mental Health Issues: Substance use disorders are correlated highly with mental health issues, some more strongly than others. They include mood disorders (major depressive disorder and bipolar disorder), thought disorders (schizophrenia), and antisocial personality disorder. Because the co-occurrence is so common, we will go into more detail around parsing out treatment options in the treatment section of this book. If you're wondering why this is the case? Hella good question with only best-guess answers. Oftentimes, the mental health issue was already showing up in someone's life, and the substances or behaviors became a way of getting some relief from them. But other times, someone with a genetic or epigenetic predisposition to a mental health issue starts using drugs or alcohol, and this activates the mental health issue.

Neurodiversity Issues: Neurodivergence diagnoses refer to differences in the brain's executive functioning. Substance use disorders also very commonly co-occur with attention deficit hyperactivity disorder and borderline personality disorder (yes, BPD is a form of neurodiversity). The world is *already* overwhelming and if you are neurodiverse even more so. So it again becomes a matter of using substances to soften the overwhelm that the brain can't process.

Trauma: At this point in my career as a mental-health author, I think listing trauma in every "why" section is part of my contract. But, yes, trauma totally belongs on this list. And because a trauma response (including PTSD) is a nervous system injury, it operates differently than other mental health diagnoses. And the way the brain processes trauma (our fear circuitry, specifically) has an enormous overlap with how the brain develops an addiction, specifically because both cause physical, structural changes to the ventral tegmental area (VTA) of the brain. The VTA is a group of neurons that sit midbrain, heavily influencing our dopamine response and interacting both with our prefrontal cortex and brainstem.

All of this is to say: this is really fucking complicated and is more than likely a perfect storm of a bunch of different influences in our lives. And also to say there is no "if you had only just . . . " answer if you are the one who is struggling. Our brains are not wired for the modern world and the easy availability of things we can use to medicate trauma, stress, loneliness, discomfort, pain, and the like. Addictions cross all borders, all ethnic groups, all levels of socioeconomic status. We're all susceptible if we happen upon our own perfect storm of who we are while living in the world that is.

What Makes It an Addiction Instead of Something Else?

So how do we operationalize "addiction?" Okie dokie. First of all? Formally, we don't use the word *addiction*. I mean . . . we all use it in regular conversation, hence the name of the book, but addiction isn't a clinical or diagnostic term. It's scientifically imprecise, which makes researchers and clinicians understandably cranky (and sometimes at odds with each other). But as psychiatry professor James Morrison points out, the word addiction comes from the terms *addicere* and *addictus,* referencing Roman law as far back as the year 5 BCE, when it was used to describe a *surrender to a master.* Anyone who has lived with and fought against an addiction is likely nodding their head in agreement.

As of this writing, if you're looking in the newest edition of the Diagnostic and Statistical Manual of Mental Disorders (DSM-5), which is what healthcare professionals use, you will see the term *substance use disorders* (SUDs).[5] And the only addiction that is not directly correlated with a particular substance (which we generally refer to as a *process addiction* or *behavioral addiction*), gambling, is referred to as a *non-substance-related disorder*.

Why the change? Excellent question, smart cookie! Historically, we focused mostly on the physical-dependence aspect of use disorders. It's what early clinicians and early peer support people (like twelve-step sponsors) could easily see and measure. So we looked for the body's experience of tolerance and withdrawal.

Tolerance refers to the physical effect of repeated use of a drug in which we stop getting relief from our original dose and need more of it. This is generally true of all kinds of substances. I need a higher dose of my asthma medication than I did twenty years ago because that's the nature of being on asthma medications the entirety of my life. But tolerance alone doesn't equal addiction. It isn't even a factor with most hallucinogens, beyond tolerance to the stimulant effect of PCP.

Withdrawal is the other important component. It means that the body physically becomes dependent on that substance to maintain stasis. Also true of all kinds of substances. To go back to my asthma medication example, I do enjoy breathing

5 Which is also the acronym for "subjective unit of distress" . . . the 0-10 scale all therapists adore using to discuss symptomatology. Yes, we *do* embrace being confusing AF with our mental health acronyms.

air, and my lungs aren't always great about that task on their own, so I need the medicine in my body. If that substance was no longer available, I'd get sick. And with some substances, like alcohol and opioids, we can get so sick that we will die without medical intervention. Other common withdrawal symptoms are incredibly uncomfortable but generally not life-threatening, including mood changes (anxiety, depression, irritability), abnormal motor activity (either immobility or extreme restlessness), sleep issues (too much or too little), and other physical issues (appetite changes, feeling exhausted). But as with tolerance, it doesn't apply to all substances. Withdrawal isn't a factor with hallucinogens (including the just-mentioned PCP) or inhalants.

In the vein of a late-night Ginsu knife commercial, I have to say it: *But wait, there's more!* If tolerance and withdrawal aren't our best tools to pinpoint a use disorder then how can we tell? A use disorder also includes the following:

Impaired Control (no longer being in charge of use):
- Using more of a substance than you planned on or more often than you planned on

- Wanting to cut down and finding yourself unable to do so

Social Problems (impact on life domains):
- Neglecting people and your responsibilities to them and yourself

- Giving up activities that you used to enjoy in order to focus more time on your use

- Inability to complete tasks you *do* set out to do because your use gets in the way

Risky Use (doing dumb shit in the name of using):
- Using in increasingly risky ways or settings

- Continuing to use despite the problems use creates

These indicators are where those of us on asthma medications or some equivalent form of medical care drop off the list. I don't have impaired control, social problems, or risky use associated with my asthma meds unless I throw my rescue inhaler at some asshole and give them a shiner, right?

These categories could easily become vague and misinterpreted, so the DSM goes more specific with eleven potential indicators of a problem, which are referred to as *diagnostic criteria*. So the diagnostic criteria in the current DSM include:

- Taking more of the substance than you intended to or using more frequently or for longer than you intended to

- Wanting to or trying to cut back but not managing to do so

- Spending more and more time on getting the substance, using it, or recovering from having used it

- Taking the substance in larger amounts or for longer than you're meant to

- Having urges or cravings to use the substance

- Not being able to keep up with the other things you are supposed to be doing in your life (work, school, home, relationships)

- Continuing to use the substance even when it is causing relationship conflict and/or problems

- Giving up important activities/things you enjoy because of the substance use

- Repeatedly using the substance even when doing so puts you in danger

- Continuing to use the substance even though you have other issues (due to physical or mental health) that get worse due to the substance use, or caused by the substance use

- Needing more of the substance to get the effect you were seeking from it

- Having withdrawal symptoms that are managed by taking more of the substance

The DSM-5 also delineates the severity of the use disorder based on the number of present symptoms. Kinda like how cancer is staged based on how it is moving through the body.

So noting that an individual is Stage 1, 2, or 3 is shorthand for saying there are 2-3 indicators present (Stage 1), 4-5 (Stage 2), 6 or more (Stage 3). Someone listed as a *Stage 1* is mild, *Stage 2* is moderate, *Stage 3* is severe.[6]

The staging of a use disorder isn't to say, *"Oh this person's use is nbd, but this person is hella fucked up,"* but to help ascertain the level of support someone will need while addressing the amount of time and level of care they may need for recovery. It's especially important if you are having to fight a health insurance behemoth about coverage of necessary treatment.

Types of Addictions

As noted, the DSM, published by the American Psychiatric Association (current version is the DSM-5-TR), is the tool we most use in the United States to diagnose both mental health and substance use disorder issues. The manual organizes substances by how they operate in the body, which is known as *classes of drugs.* The only non-substance that is considered an addiction is gambling and why *that* one is included but others are not will be unpacked in a bit. The specific substance categories in the DSM are the following:

Alcohol

Caffeine

Cannabis

Hallucinogens

6 You may also see, in certain spaces, the term Stage .5, meaning someone's use has positioned them to be at risk for a use disorder.

Phencyclidine (and similarly acting arylcyclohexylamines and other hallucinogens)

Inhalants

Opioids

Sedatives

Hypnotics

Anxiolytics

Stimulants (amphetamine-type substances, cocaine, and other stimulants)

Tobacco

Other/Unknown Substances (which is often used for noting anabolic steroids, nitrous oxide, other prescription and OTC drugs, and the like)

. . . and finally, the one behavioral addiction: gambling.

And within these main categories are a lot of more specific diagnoses. Like over three hundred of them. From what type of substance to what type of problems the substance is causing, and even the timing of the substance use with the problems that are being experienced.[7] Why so much detail? Keep in mind that the DSM is meant to be a communication

---

7 Clinicians? This is another good reason to go through your diagnostic manual with the client. It's empowering for everyone to be actively involved in the diagnostic process and lessens chances of biffing the diagnosis, when so much else about access to care rests on us getting it right.

shorthand between professionals for the purpose of treatment.

It is designed to shorten the process of demonstrating, "This is what's going on that is causing enormous pain in their lives and we're trying to help them manage the illness and recover their lives . . . and while YMMV this will give you a solid starting point on treatment planning, support, and care for a human being who is struggling right now."

So it DOES really suck when the limitations of the DSM make it a struggle to receive care, get care covered by our insurance provider, and the like. The DSM was never meant to exist as the gatekeeping tool, but it has become so because capitalism + supremely flawed healthcare systems = fuck you, prove you deserve treatment.

Gambling: A Process Addiction

When we think of gambling, we think of the traditional methods like playing poker or betting on the ponies. However, technology is creating new ways for our un-modern brains to get hooked in, and it also makes sense to consider (and start researching) how some things that seem to fall under the "shopping" category may be lighting us up in a way similar to other gambling behaviors. The European Union started stricter regulations around gaming loot boxes and the like for just this reason. If the behavior has a risk/reward ratio that is different from simply spending too much at the mall, we need to take into consideration that this might be an issue.

We can see the difference in the brain of someone who has taken drugs right? It's "lit up" in a way that is different from someone unaltered (or, at least, as unaltered as a human being in modern society can be). A fuck-ton of research shows that gambling behaviors function like a substance addiction; whereas, shopping behaviors simply do not light up the brain in the same way. While shopping behaviors are efficiently treated with the same protocols that are used to treat mood disorders (like cognitive behavioral therapy [CBT] and antidepressants), individuals who are addicted to gambling don't respond to those treatments effectively. The recidivism rate for gambling addiction is really high (about 75 percent . . . and that's with the understanding that only about 20 percent of people who have a gambling addiction seek treatment to begin with). That is likely a function of the fact that the people who experienced a relapse weren't being treated effectively; SSRIs and cognitive-based therapies are incredibly helpful for treating these co-occurring issues but not the gambling itself, which responds best to the real, efficacious, addictions-based treatments that reflect what's really going on in the brain (what that includes is discussed later in the book, promise).

Gambling addiction criteria are slightly different because gambling is behavioral, but the criteria will still seem very similar to those for substance addictions:

- Spending more and more money when gambling in order to achieve the same excitement as before

- Restlessness and irritability when you have tried to stop gambling or decrease your gambling

- Repeated unsuccessful attempts to stop gambling or decrease your gambling

- Thinking about gambling frequently, such as planning your next gambling experience, mentally revisiting previous experiences, and focusing on ways of getting money so you can gamble again

- When you don't feel well emotionally, you are far more likely to gamble

- If you lose money gambling, you want to gamble more in order to even out your losses ("chasing" one's losses)

- Relying on others to help with gambling-related money problems

- Lying to conceal your gambling activities

- Your gambling has significantly affected another life domain in a negative way, such as losing or jeopardizing a relationship, a job, or an educational opportunity

Changes from the DSM-IV to the DSM-5

So as I alluded to above, the current version of the DSM, the DSM-5 (or DSM-5-TR—the revised version that was released in the middle of me writing this book . . . RUDE) made some useful changes to diagnosing use disorders. In the previous version, there were two separate diagnoses: substance abuse and substance dependence. And that is such a difficult thing to parse out correctly. And it means people who could haven received appropriate care early weren't "sick enough" to do so.

Remember all the criteria from above and how the diagnosis is supposed to be in stages? The DSM-IV only required one symptom to be present for a diagnosis, and while even one symptom merits concern, using one criteria to lay a pretty heavy diagnosis on someone is a very dick move.

There was also one big diagnostic criteria change. The legal problems criteria ("More than once gotten arrested, been held at a police substation, or had other legal problems because of your drinking") was removed. Because, let's face it, some people are incredibly well insulated from the consequences of their actions. In fact, many of them just continue to hold public office. The replacement criteria, which is far more universal, is about cravings and/or a strong desire to use ("wanted to drink so badly you couldn't think of anything else").

The DSM-5 also eliminated two things. The first was the option of a polysubstance dependence, which was used when someone was using two or more substances and experiencing some problems surrounding their use but not enough problems to warrant an addiction diagnosis for any one substance. The idea was that, in aggregate, it constituted an addiction but research didn't back that up or find that the diagnosis was predictive in preventing more severe problems later.

The second elimination was of the physiological-dependence subtype, which was used to delineate when our body becomes used to having the substance in its system and struggles to function without it. Physiological dependence has also been found to not be predictive of a substance use disorder so why fuck with semantics if it doesn't matter?

Mental Health Issues That Commonly Co-Occur with Addiction

At a population level, about half of us who misuse alcohol, street drugs, or prescription drugs also have at least one mental health disorder. That number gets even higher for certain ethnic groups; for example, about three-quarters of the people indigenous to Turtle Island have co-occurring disorders. In fact, depression and diabetes so commonly occur with an alcohol use disorder among Indigenous folks, it even has a name: triADD. Some of these conditions are independent of the addiction, and others are often related (or even brought on by) the substance use, especially depression, anxiety, and sudden-onset psychosis.

Historically, the treatment approach was "get sober and then we will sort out the rest." There are still people that I (otherwise) really admire in our field who feel this way. And in case that sentence didn't signal the punch, I adamantly do not.

Now, someone who is in a medical crisis because of their substance use (including a detox that requires medical oversight, like with opiates or alcohol) shouldn't be left to vomit in the corner while getting CBT for depression. But more and more clinicians and programs are recognizing that there should be no gatekeeping to providing care. We call this the "no wrong door" approach. If you roll in for depression treatment and the substance use is there, that care should be provided or coordinated on your behalf. And if you roll in for substance use treatment and depression is there? Same-same.

That being said? Some of what looks like a mental health issue is hugely substance-related and may resolve with recovery. What do we look for? Damn, you are so sharp with the questions today, good one! Let's unpack:

- The chicken or the egg? Did the mental health disorder start first or the substance use? Many people turn to substances to medicate the pain of an untreated mental health issue. Bipolar disorder, schizophrenia, and antisocial personality disorder are commonly showing their ass in our lives before the substance use begins.

- How fast was the onset of the mental health symptoms? Like did they start hella quick or have they been building slowly over time? Hella quick can be a sign that it's related to the toxins building up in the body from the substances.

- If sobriety is achieved, and the mental health issue doesn't resolve or greatly diminish within thirty days, it's quite likely independent of the substance use, which entirely makes sense, right?

- A diagnostician will likely want to see more active symptoms of a mental health issue rather than fewer if a substance use is also present. This may feel like "great, I have to be sick AF to get diagnosed???" but that isn't the case at all. It's about not overdiagnosing if the cause of your symptoms are a little sus. A couple symptoms of an anxiety disorder coupled with substance use could be anxiety or could be the substance. A bunch of symptoms of an anxiety disorder are far more likely to be an independent mental health issue.

- If it's all a jumbled mess with a confusing timelines (cuz, life) . . . a good clinician can tag the symptoms as "unspecified whatever" (like unspecified anxiety disorder, unspecified mood disorder) or list rule-outs (often charted as r/o's) to be considered as other healing work progresses.

WHAT ABOUT OUT OF CONTROL BEHAVIORS?

A lot of what's portrayed as process addictions are better described as out of control behaviors (OCBs). And let me back up a bit and apologize for a previous linguistic choice. In my bestseller *Unfuck Your Brain*, I refer to hard and soft addictions. Hard addictions being the ones listed in the DSM and soft addictions meaning things that are causing huge life difficulties but don't have an actual DSM diagnosis. But weird shit has happened in intervening years regarding these problem behaviors. While there have always been people providing shady services around fake health needs, this particular corner of the field got terrifyingly scary.

The NoFap movement, designed to break cis-het men of sex and porn "addiction," developed stronger and stronger ties to far-right ideology and movements such as the Proud Boys and 4chan and its various doppelgangers. If you are thinking, "Seriously . . . wait, what?" I'm with you. It essentially became a mechanism for showing how macho you should be. Not a "Hey, it's not a great use of your time to be wanking to porn all damn day . . . go learn a new language or go to a cooking class or something." But as in, "Don't masturbate, like at all." You've heard of "No Nut November?" Yep, these tiki-torch wielding jackwagons think they are far more manly if they don't ever have a wank. And it has nothing to do with some twisted notion of respecting women.[8] In NoFap, people who masterbate are called coomers (a portmanteau of *boomer* and *coming*) because they are weak soyboys giving up all the testosterone they need to stay manly.

And then comes the "research" they use to back up their claims. But it's research that falls apart once you know what to look for. Reading any kind of research takes a critical eye, sex research even more so. There isn't room enough for a rant of the scope it would take to go through all of their talking points so I won't try to, at least not in this book.

So let me just say the following instead:

- None of the rigorous research in the field backs up any of the meta-messages of this movement.

- I have seen, as a clinician, the harm caused to individuals who bought into these ideas (and maybe even sought expensive treatments at facilities that embody these practices), which I then have to help them . . . unfuck.

- Deciding that these activities are not good for you-the-individual-person may be entirely appropriate

8 You can absolutely enjoy erotic performance and still respect women. It starts with paying the content creators for their work instead of downloading it for free. I do enjoy some sexy respect.

for any number of reasons. Which is something a competent therapist can help you figure out. But deciding what is right for other people, when there isn't evidence that demonstrates you are correct, is a dick move. Pun absolutely intended.

All this to say that the politicization and resulting harm has led me to move away from the term "soft addiction" to the term used by Douglas Braun-Harvey and Michael A. Vigorito to describe issues with sex and porn. They use the term *out of control sexual behavior*. Their work in treating problems with sex and porn are explained in their excellent book, *Treating Out of Control Sexual Behavior: Rethinking Sex Addiction*, and both teach courses on the subject.[9]

Loss of control generally refers to the experience of overwhelming emotion leading to a lack of *proactive* decision making. In a clinical sense, however, it can also refer to our human experience of *feeling* that our decision-making ability has been hijacked by our own internal processes, and we don't know how to regain ourselves, even if nothing we are doing is being perceived as dangerous or problematic.

That was a lengthy explanation for a linguistic choice, but I think it's an important one. With the caveat that if further research demonstrates that sex and porn usage (or any other behavior that we perceive as being out of control behavior) does operate like an addiction, I will say "my bad" once again

---

9 Two other excellent and highly recommended books that speak to sex and porn work specifically are David Ley's *The Myth of Sex Addiction* and *Ethical Porn for Dicks* if you wanna read up.

and correct my work. I'm fine with that. I'm wrong at least three times before I even get out of bed in the morning, so it would be nothing new.

But not talking about common issues that many individuals struggle with would be shitty and unhelpful to the people who read my books in hopes of finding understanding, resources, and support. So it's super important to include at least the most common OCBs. The DSM-5 inclusion of a "process addiction" section, which currently only contains gambling addiction, has opened the doors to more research in the area. It may very well end up expanding.

The authors and committee members responsible for the DSM-5 noted that many repetitive behaviors perceived as problematic are being studied for possible inclusion but are not yet supported as having the same underlying mechanisms as what we are clinically terming addictions. Which means the appropriate standard of care is to consider strategies for managing what feels out of control while treating the underlying issue the behavior was developed to compensate for. As we start talking about treatment options later in this book, you will see how different the evidence-based practices are for someone using porn problematically versus someone struggling mightily with a substance use disorder.

Where Out of Control Behaviors Come From

I have too many rescue cats. At current count? Four. Four rescue cats. Which is ridiculous, I know. But four is better than seven.

Three of them were rescued as kittens, and the fourth I rescued as an adult. So she has more trauma history than the others and struggles mightily at times. When she is activated/dysregulated she has a tendency to punch or bite the human she is sitting on. Meaning me, most of the time.

And meaning she is cuddled on my lap of her own accord taking a nap while I work, then her brain yells "DANGER" and she freaks out and punches me in the face. She often doesn't even leave after doing so, just goes back to sleep. Punching and biting are *short-term energy relieving behaviors* (STERBs). It is something she does impulsively. A rapid, unplanned reaction. It helps her feel better in the moment so she can relax again.

Would you say she has a punching and biting addiction? It fits the criteria just as well as any of the other "behavioral addictions," doesn't it? A rapid, unplanned action that we feel we have no control over? But it also seems like a bizarrely unhelpful way of framing an adaptive behavior, doesn't it?

And okay, she's a cat. So she wouldn't have a 12-step program to attend. But what if she was a traumatized human who lashed out in such a manner? Would we start with *"I admit that I am powerless over punching and biting, and my life has become unmanageable?"* Punching and biting are actually important responses for a cat to have in certain situations; we aren't looking to change her ability to protect herself when need be.

So we figure out how to help her control her behavior and learn healthier coping skills while figuring out what causes her nervous system to go haywire in certain situations.

And I am happy to report that the number of times my cat has punched or bit me has decreased so dramatically that I can tell you exactly how many times it happens each year. Last year was only three punches and *no* bites. She's in recovery.

When we are talking about behaviors that are or that feel like they are "out of control," we are talking about struggling with a level of impulsivity, which researchers in the field have noted is as complex and multifaceted a construct as anything else we are trying to tease apart. Professor of psychiatry F.G. Moeller[10] and colleagues defined impulsivity as "a predisposition toward rapid, unplanned reactions to internal or external stimuli [with diminished] regard to the negative consequences of these reactions to the impulsive individual or to others."

Meaning . . . we feel out of control of our own actions.

I've written about STERBs in other books; we talk about this term often in grief research, though any emotion that is uncomfortable can create an impulse to STERB. Because it gives us a bit of relief, if just for the time being. And yes, you will absolutely see researchers that posit that any impulsive behaviors that can be harmful, excessive, or otherwise causing

---

10 I am a fan of anyone who has the first and middle initials F.G. btw.

life difficulties must be addictions. And while there are some overlaps in neurobiology (because anything that feels good lights up the brain in similar ways), we don't have enough data to determine if the pathophysiology (the mechanism of the development of a disease) is indeed the same.

Brain mapping in this area is still really new, but really interesting. It seems that out of control behaviors are impacted by the sensorimotor putamen (involved in movement regulation) and the associative caudate (involved with the accuracy of memory and connections we hold in our memory). In one study of out of control eating behaviors, the individuals in question had fewer dopamine receptors in the brain and less dopamine in general. So the out of control behaviors may be related not to getting extra dopamine but striving for the amount one sees in a "normal, healthy" brain. So it seems that problematic behaviors aren't creating a high, they're creating a baseline normal.

Additionally, human behavior researchers have determined that the human need for control is innate, not learned. And having choices helps us perceive a sense of control in our lives, which helps us moderate and manage stress. Once our STERBs seem to be causing a relinquishment of control rather than an opportunity to have control, we feel a sense of disintegration.

How does this relate to neuroscience? Psychologist Daryl Bem termed our internal process in this regard a facet of *self-perception theory*. He noted that the way humans unpack their own mindsets, emotions, and behaviors is the same way we try to understand it in others, by making presumptions about our behaviors. Dr. Bem said we don't really look at our emotions and cognitions, just our behaviors. And use only our *behaviors* to make decisions about our internal world. As in, *"If I don't feel in control of myself, it is because I am not."* Which is why I am focusing, over and over, on the importance of unpacking the underlying issues, especially around out of control behaviors, because that part is so often missing from treatment planning and recovery work.

Types of Out of Control Behaviors

Anything that has the capacity to stimulate our brains and bodies can be addictive. Tolerance and withdrawal aside, anything that provides some kind of positive effect or relief puts us in danger of it becoming an obligation or a need instead of a choice or habit. If you feel that this is an uncomfortably broad approach, I agree. We like to like things. Our brains lighting up feels good. I like cooking. And taking new classes to challenge myself. And looking at Christmas lights. And blasting music in my car.

No one that I am aware of considers any of those things addictions, but other things I might mention could make a behaviorist's brow furrow. Like saying I adore ice cream and working out and shopping for books and using my cellphone to chat with my friends. And sex? Definitely. These are the behaviors that are being most studied as possible process addictions. So let's look at the research around these out of control behaviors and unpack what we know.

Food/Sugar

The idea of food addiction has been around since the fifties (that's the middle of the twentieth century, my young ones). Today, the concept of food addiction is another big one that you will see talked about on social media. In fact, 86 percent of Americans believe that certain foods have addictive qualities, and 72 percent believe that these addictive qualities account for some cases of obesity.

Sugar is the big one we think we're addicted to. And yes, it is true that humans do have an evolutionary preference for sweetness and a weaker off-switch when it comes to sugar. Sweet foods were a rarity in early human history (like stumbling upon a bramble of ripe berries when out foraging or hunting) and they are energy-dense. So we developed the ability to detect these mono- and disaccharide food sources readily and likely can eat more of them when they are available in order to store that energy for later.

So a sugar addiction would make evolutionary sense. But . . . that's not what the problem is. It turns out that it is higher fat foods, both sweet and savory, that researchers have consistently found to be the problem for people who are overeating in ways that we may consider addictive. Even if sweets are your bag, it's the ice cream and cookies (fat and sugar and flavor!) not sugar straight from the sugar jar.

If certain foods are able to hijack the reward systems in our brain, blocking those reward signals would have some effect, as they do with drugs. ΔFosB (Delta FosB) is a regulatory protein in the human body that has been found to play a significant role in the development and maintenance of chemical addiction. If your body tends to overexpress this protein, you are more likely to fall down the addiction rabbit hole. However, ΔFosB has not been connected with foods in humans. Blocking dopamine function has been tested and found to be ineffective in managing what we have termed food addiction for going on a century now. Using an opioid blocker has also proven unhelpful.

Essentially, as far as researchers have found (at the time of me writing this) there is no neurobiological underpinning for food addiction based on how we understand and measure addiction. The scale used to measure food addiction is likely measuring a subtype of binge eating disorder instead.

Shopping

Shopping addiction? Is that a real thing?

Do you buy way too much dumb shit? Or maybe it's cool shit, but in amounts that are kind of embarrassing (says the person who owns every gray sweater ever manufactured in her size).

Are you worried that your shopping may be a problem? Sure, it could be . . . but maybe not in the way that you think.

Shopping is a symptom of other shit going on in a person's life. Compulsive Buying Disorder generally runs in families and exists with another diagnosis, like mood disorders, anxiety disorders, eating disorders, and other impulse disorders.

Survey-based research shows that about 6 to 16 percent of any first-world population would qualify as compulsive buyers. These same surveys also demonstrate that 80 to 95 percent of individuals who qualify as "compulsive buyers" are women, though that's likely a survey design problem. Interestingly, most research reviews on compulsive buying have noted the same thing that I have noticed in my practice . . . that men are far more likely to call themselves "collectors" or use any other word than "shopper." So if you find that while you don't have a compulsive buying disorder, you do over-collect gray sweaters (ahem), this may still apply to you.

Compulsive buying patterns have been studied, and people who engage in the behavior generally report feeling negative emotions (anger, depression, anxiety, self-criticism, boredom) that are alleviated when they make a new purchase. The overlap varies from study to study, but one study I read showed that literally 100 percent of the people with compulsive buying behaviors also had a mood disorder.

Shopping can provide a feeling of relief from the fuckitude of the other stuff people are feeling. It's considered a STERB and gives us a sense of control when we feel out of control.

So it makes sense that there isn't a generalized pattern of out of control shopping. Managing shopping behaviors happens when we manage the underlying fuckitude. There are studies that show treating depression in people with problematic shopping behaviors also causes remission of the problematic shopping behavior. Using cognitive behavior therapy techniques to identify and manage the negative thoughts that activate the shopping impulse has been shown to be effective for the same reason.

When we can recognize, "I feel like shit and utterly powerless" and work with those thoughts and feelings, we are far less likely to medicate them with impulsive behavior, whether that behavior is texting selfies to an ex for attention, vaguebooking continuously, picking fights with friends, or buying our seventh pair of black boots that we absolutely do not need (except for the fact that they go great with the gray sweaters!). Remember that compulsive buying is a symptom of other stuff going on, and you deserve real healing.

Exercise

In the sixties and seventies, mental health clinicians and researchers became interested in the idea of "positive addictions," meaning things we can't really overdo because they are really good for us. Exercise was the prime example until researcher William Morgan pointed out in 1979 that exercise may not be a positive addiction because of how it can create injury and change life domain functioning. And the seed for considering exercise an addiction was born.

One of the biggest issues with how "exercise addiction" was measured is that the focus tends to be on elite athletes. The intensity of athletic training for these athletes is unquestioned. However, the main tool used to measure exercise addiction (the aptly named Exercise Addiction Inventory [EAI]) being applied to exercise creates problems of interpretation. Yes, they have to work out and practice substantially. It's their job. So statements on the inventory like, "Exercise is the most important thing in my life" may be completely true since athletics is an elite athlete's job. "Conflicts have arisen between me and my family and/or my partner about the amount of exercise I do" may also be entirely true, especially if one's partner is not an elite athlete and would probably like to watch movies and eat popcorn with their elite athlete partner more than they do. Even the index statement, "If I have to miss an exercise session I feel moody and irritable" makes complete sense because training sessions are required to participate in competitions.

So you see how this diagnostic inventory won't work for everyone.

Okay, fine, you're thinking. What about us normies who just like to hit the gym or the trails? What about when that becomes too much? A well-designed study demonstrates other problems with the exercise addiction "diagnosis." Like with shopping, studies demonstrate that when the EAI is provided along with depression inventories, body dysmorphia inventories, and eating disorder inventories . . .

the correlations become pretty clear. Depression accounts for a lot of the over-exercising behaviors, but the biggest culprit is disordered eating and body image issues. Meaning the exercising is about burning calories and changing or managing the shape of one's body . . . not the positive health benefits that one gets from the exercise itself.

Sex and Porn

High sex drive, porn usage, masturbation, cheating, and other behaviors around sex have been increasingly attributed to sex addiction over recent decades. Sex addiction is a multi-billion dollar treatment industry . . . and it's based on something that literally doesn't exist.

I have many people come to see me because their behavior regarding sex or porn is really pissing off their partner. The word "addiction" starts getting thrown around, and the do-er gets an ultimatum that shit's over if they don't get therapy for their "problem."

Can you engage in sex (partnered or solo, porn-enhanced or not) in a way that is problematic? Sure. But there is one thing that needs to be said first: wanting sex, enjoying sex, and being excited about sex does not make you a sex addict. Having cheated on a partner means you did something shitty to someone you love, but it doesn't make you a sex addict. Wanting porn, enjoying porn, and being excited about porn does not make you a porn addict.

Let me say that one more time for the people in the back: being sex and porn positive does not an addiction make. Alfred Kinsey once remarked, "A nymphomaniac is someone who has more sex than you do." When the brain lights up in the process of doing something like gambling, it's easy to see the reward circuit being activated in a way it doesn't for someone who doesn't share that process addiction. But sex (solo or partnered) is *supposed to* light up the reward centers of the brain. Everyone's brains light up that way. So can you safely label it an addiction? No.

More research on better mechanisms for diagnosis are needed. But since we don't yet have a "sex addiction" blood test or brain scan test to rely on, figuring out problematic sexual behavior is individual and contextual. And it's one of those places where a well-trained, sex-positive therapist can be of benefit. For example, like with the shopping "addiction" example above? When it turned out that everyone in one study that was engaging in compulsive buying had a mood disorder? And once it was treated the compulsive shopping behavior faded on its own? Out of control sexual behavior has a huge overlap with attention-deficit-hyperactivity-disorder (ADHD), which is yet another reason why screening for neurodiversity is a necessary part of therapeutic care. There is also a huge overlap with other life domain stressors, and it often "self-corrects" when care and consideration are provided around those stressors.

I don't know anyone who likes what they are doing when they do this. Not past the immediate moment of engagement, anyway. And they don't like *themselves* all that much, either. Because their behavior is separating them from all the amazing, messy, authentic, beautiful relationships the world has to offer, it's no longer aligned with their values and keeps them from prioritizing the people they love. That's what defines a problem.

If you are worried that your solo sex activities are problematic to your partnered sex (or if your partner states that they are), it's important to unpack the impetus of the behavior and the effect it's having on your other life domains. Generally speaking, when you are dealing with the other stressors in your life effectively, this "problem" takes care of itself.

If you realize that your current sexual activities are posing a problem for you, then it may be of benefit to get some support. One of the biggest problems in this area is the number of clinicians profiting on the stigma and shame surrounding sex. Which means that doing careful research is really important. Ask any therapists that you are interested in seeing what their stance on sex addiction and porn usage is.

If you are dealing with past religious or cultural messages around your sex and pornography usage, ask them if they are comfortable with helping you explore that without adding their own value system to the conversation. I recently read an article *by a therapist* who views masturbation as a form of spousal abuse. Yes, literally. There is enough shame and stigma around sex out there as it is. You sure as fuck don't need it from your therapist.

Tech

In the eighties and nineties there were rumblings about "television addiction" and "amusement machine addiction" (video games I guess?). Then the internet, designed for the military but quickly privatized for fun stuff, became ubiquitous. And in the past decade or so, most of us have moved to carrying the internet in our pocket at all times. A new potential problem, Internet Addiction Disorder (IAD) was born.

But generally speaking, the more rigorous research says, "Nah," noting that the formulation of IAD was based on other addiction pathologies and were ill-suited to determining if tech was addictive in-and-of-itself. The definitions and constructs involved were found to be "broad and generic," therefore not helpful in determining if something is causing distraction, discomfort, or distress.

And the research around specific tech addictions, like "internet addiction" and "gaming addiction" show the same underlying causes: depression, anxiety, low self-worth, loneliness, and shyness. Meaning people reaching out for comfort, care, and companionship. I wrote about this very issue in my book *Unfuck Your Friendships*. In 2009, researchers Jaye Derrick, Shira Gabriel, and Kurt Hugenberg developed the *Social Surrogacy Hypothesis*. They looked at multiple studies that found that these online (and sometimes parasocial[11]) relationships serve to buffer us against loneliness and the assorted mental and physical health issues that can occur when we experience chronic loneliness. The research on being online and connecting with others through online platforms encourages us to use it as a waystation. Meaning connecting through social media so you can build from there, connecting with people one-on-one and hopefully in person. Like joining a local hiking group on Facebook then actually meeting everyone for a weekend hike. Or joining a local Zoom support group and exchanging numbers with someone else in the group who you really want to spend more time with. If you are a queer punk in Podunk, Arkansas, meeting others face-to-face may not be possible, but moving from surface chatter and photo-liking into having individual and authentic online connections with others can benefit your mental health instead of making it worse.

Now, that being said? The other diagnostic tool that clinicians use is the International Classification of Diseases (ICD), which is published by the World Health Organization (WHO). Where the DSM is in its fifth iteration complete with a full text revision, the ICD is in its eleventh form. And

---

11 Parasocial relationships are the types of relationships when we feel a sense of connection with a public figure or someone else we admire and only engage with through social media. Like we aren't friends-friends, but we have a sense that we know a lot about their lives, and we care about their wellbeing. This isn't a bad thing, it's a human thing. Parasocial relationships can help support a lonely person and can be used to influence others into making good choices (like the influencer who encourages everyone to recycle their soda cans or whatever). Parasocial relationships are discussed in more detail in my book *Unfuck Your Friendships*.

there is an addiction included in it that is not in the DSM: gaming disorder, referring specifically to video gaming and/or digital gaming.

This is where it gets interesting. The World Health Organization states that gaming disorder needs to be better standardized than it is now. Which, hard agree. Many of the issues associated with gaming are issues with microtransactions and loot boxes within the games themselves. If this is totally out of your realm of experience like it was for me, it means that the games encourage you to make purchases to use within the platform. These purchases are often "blind," meaning you don't know if you are going to get what you are hoping for or, like Charlie Brown, a rock. Hence, it is a form of *gambling* creating the problem, not *gaming*. Should this be the case, treatment protocols used for gambling addiction make far more sense than any others.

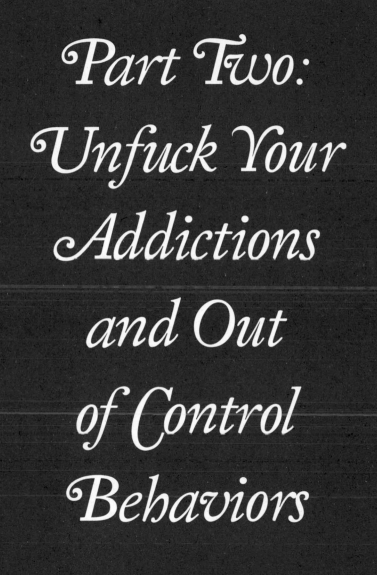

Part Two: Unfuck Your Addictions and Out of Control Behaviors

CONSIDERING AND MAKING CHANGES

The Relational Recovery List

I first published this list in my addiction chapter of my book *Unfuck Your Brain*. As a relational-cultural (RCT) trained therapist, I view my clinical work (including addictions recovery work) through a relational frame. Yes, this will seem very similar to a traditional twelve-step list. I wasn't looking to replace it, just reframe it through the lens of connection.

This is clearly the world according to Dr. Faith. I am no more right or wrong than anyone else, but I have been doing this work for a very long time and have found ways of supporting recovery that work best for the individuals I work with and my own worldview and treatment style.

Now, anyone who says they have the BEST way to treat addiction is a fucking liar. I would never claim such nonsense. So take my suggestions for only what they are—suggestions. Use anything that works for you and dump the rest.

1. Consider addiction's rightful place in your life as being a replacement relationship.

Shit ends up in the addiction zone when it starts replacing our authentic relationships with the people around us and with our own selves. In other words, we end up serving the substance or behavior instead of ourselves and the people we care about. It isn't just a thing in our life, it becomes the *most important* thing in our life. Addiction recovery is a recognition of that. Maybe you don't feel that you have any relationships worth saving. Maybe you don't even think that YOU are worth saving. I'd beg to differ, but it's not up to me. I would suggest, gentle reader, that you give space to the possibility that there are good relationships out there to be had. And your current addiction is a nasty, dirty bitch who is never gonna love you back the way you deserve to be loved. When you are hanging out with your addiction, consider what needs are being met and if this is really the ideal way of handling them. Once we become conscious of our engagement with the addiction and remind ourselves we are choosing the addiction over ourselves and over others, it becomes harder and harder to continue to make that choice. Don't step into your use without being mindful of what you are doing. It gets harder and harder to fuck over yourself and the people you love when you are doing it with intentionality and ownership.

2. You're in charge of yourself. You really are. Even if you feel that you aren't. Even if you feel that you never have been.

Ultimately, your use will change because you want it to. You will change because you want to be better, because you want your relationships to be better. Even if you get remanded by a court into treatment, whether or not you stay sober will ultimately be up to how badly you want to, right? No matter what people tell you to do, whether or not you do it is ultimately up to you. Remind yourself of that when you feel yourself bristling against authority. What do YOU want for yourself? Is what you are doing getting you there?

3. It's far easier to START doing something new than STOP doing something old.

A lot of really great clinicians are fearful of working with individuals with addictions because they think the idea is to get someone to stop doing something. I take the opposite approach, focusing on adding healthier behaviors and building healthier relationships rather than focusing on the addiction itself. We may build awareness around some of the history and/or behaviors surrounding use, but we don't generally focus on the use itself. If you build a healthier you, the addiction often becomes less and less needed as a coping skill. I was asked recently, "How often does therapy consist of just getting people to get out more?" And the answer is? A helluva lot!!! You don't have to go balls to the walls superhealthypants, but can you add in one small thing that makes you feel better instead of worse every day? And can you pay attention to how you feel when doing THAT thing instead of the addiction thing?

4. Remember that sobriety and recovery are spectrums.

You get to choose the best point for yourself on that spectrum and you get to choose when that changes. Do abstinence if that works for you. Do taper + harm reduction if that works better. Part of your journey is figuring out who you are and who you can be in relation to your addiction. I have worked with people who soon learned that playing a game of poker would spiral into heroin use within a month. Only complete abstinence kept them safe. Then I have worked with other people who tapered hard drug use with marijuana. A few gave up the marijuana too at a later point (it isn't legal in the state I live in, so using had some inherent risk) and some continued to use marijuana instead of other drugs successfully for years with no relapse. As alluded to in mentioning the legality of marijuana in my state? You are, of course, responsible for all the consequences of your behavior. For example, if you are mandated to go in for drug screenings and you pop hot, you can't blame this book.

5. Stop the bullshit.

With yourself, with others. Blowing smoke up people's asses, convincing yourself that you are making good decisions when you know very fucking well that you aren't? Stop that. You may not have had much control over your life up until this point but consider this my permission slip to you to TAKE IT BACK. Accountability through and through. If you engage in your addiction, own it with honesty. Don't blame anyone else. Remind yourself that your engagement in your addiction is a choice you are making. Make it consciously. Instead of telling yourself, "My partner broke up with me so it's their fault I'm using. I just can't handle all this," try this instead, "My partner broke up with me and that triggered all my struggles with abandonment. I'm choosing to use because it's the coping skill that has worked best for me and trying something new feels overwhelming." You may find it harder to hurt yourself with your addiction when you take a mindful sense of responsibility for it.

6. Figure out your triggers.

If you squeeze your eyes shut, you will continue to bump into shit. If you keep your eyes open to the terrain, you can start putting together a map. When you catch yourself doing the thing, ask yourself to retrace what led to it. The HALT acronym is a big one in addiction treatment . . . am I hungry? Angry? Lonely? Tired? If you pair awareness triggers with accountability for your actions it becomes increasingly hard to stay on the addiction path.

7. Forgive yourself your fuck-ups.

You are a fuck-up. So am I. Yay for being human. Have some self-compassion for that fact. Self-compassion is the opposite of self-esteem. It's about your insides rather than your successes and failures on the outsides. It means you forgive yourself your failures and your human bumbling. And no, this doesn't mean you get to be a hedonistic fuck-face. In fact, if you are aware of your human frailty, and take care of yourself in the moments where you are your most fragile and off-kilter, research shows you actually take more responsibility and accountability for your actions. Kristen Neff wrote an amazing book called *Self-Compassion*. Read the thing if you haven't. Changed my life.

8. And forgive the fuck-ups done unto you.

I hear you. Some terrible shit has happened to you. Seriously awful stuff. Awful stuff will continue to happen. Sometimes people are just as balls as can be. Forgiveness isn't about them, it's about how much bullshit you want to carry around with you. I'm guessing not that fucking much. Forgiveness doesn't mean allowing ongoing dickitude. Instead, it will help you set better boundaries so you know how to better protect yourself in the future. And it will open the door to more real conversations with the people around you, instead of continuing to only converse with your demons.

9. Anticipate your continued imperfect humaning.

Do your best to do your best. But seriously. You're gonna fuck up. You may even relapse. And you know what? We either win or we learn. So take the fuck-ups as new ways of getting good information about yourself. What did you do differently this time? What can you take from this experience and do differently next time? Honoring our fuck-ups with clarity is brave as fuck. And you *so* have every capacity to be brave.

What Determines "Bad Enough"?

Back in 2004 a research article came out called "The Peculiar Longevity of Things Not So Bad," in which researchers explored an idea called the **region-beta paradox.**

Human brains have a lot of nifty tricks that can be brilliant for our survival in some instances and chaos-inducing in others. First of all, humans are able to guess about consequences, which is termed *affective forecasting.* That is, we can look at a situation we have never been in before and make a guess about how it will play out. Figuring out a crocodile doesn't want pat-pats is an example of smart affective forecasting. But there are also many quirky paradoxes our brain has developed that cause these systems to not work as effectively. Which brings us back to the region-beta paradox. The example the study authors use to demonstrate the paradox is a simple one. Say you have the choice of either walking or riding your bike for transportation, and your goal is to arrive somewhere quickly. We may choose to walk if it's fairly close or ride our bike if it seems longer.

However, riding our bike is almost always the faster option unless we are just strolling next door. Makes sense, right?

The team showed evidence that we do the same thing when guessing about life changes and emotional fallout. Here's the thing. If something is *really fucking bad* we kick into a different mode. It means we hit a certain point of pain where our tolerance is tapped out. This is called the *critical threshold*.

Which means that we recover more quickly and have less distress if something is really fucking bad. Getting a DUI may be a critical threshold, because that's some serious shit, but then we go, "Oh HELL NO" and fix it. And we feel empowered. We are sad and scared and all of those things for a while but we recover.

But when things are just kinda bad? Like you are getting fussed at for being late to work and sluggish because you're constantly hung over? Things are ungreat but tolerable for days, weeks, and months. Our drinking is kinda a problem, but we haven't missed work over it (yet). We're checked out with video games more often than not, but the basics are still getting done (so far). We don't hit a critical threshold. We just continue to deal with a sort-of bad situation. And the outcome is more harmful and causes more emotional damage in the long term.

None of this is to say you should dip on any situation that isn't perfect. Life is complicated. School, jobs, friendships, families, partnerships. We don't throw away the beautiful parts of our existence over flaws. We'd have nothing left, including ourselves if that was the case.

But when I see clients stuck in their decision-making process around "Is it bad enough to make a big change?" we start getting granular around the collective impact it's actually having on their lives. If it's stepping out of a situation, we start thinking about what *done* looks like. When do you know you need to leave this situation entirely? And how can you best and most safely extract yourself?

If that isn't a practical solution at that moment, we may look at what boundaries can be set up or what accommodations can be made to help soften some of the edges of the issue. If you can't skip out on visiting your hometown, for example, can you preserve some of your peace by renting a room so you don't have to stay with family? If you're dealing with chronic pain, can we investigate some strategies that may mitigate it enough that you can do the things that are important to you?

And you may be thinking right now, "Cool story, Doc . . . but how do I figure out if that's what's going on with my life?" which is an important and entirely valid question. So here are some questions for consideration.

1) If there was a no-muss, no-fuss easy button for you to exit this situation would you use it?

2) Do you hold up what is bothering you against someone else's "bigger problem" as a way of minimizing your experience? Important note on this one: Gaining perspective by comparing to other situations can be helpful, but *discounting* your

own experience when comparing it to others can be a problem.

3) Do you notice yourself doing a lot of wishful planning? As in "once I stop drinking" or "once I get that promotion" type of wishing? Things that haven't happened yet/ever or things that have been vaguely mentioned but without a commitment and a timeline?

4) If things are bad, but not "bad enough," what would make them bad enough to motivate you to make changes?

5) If someone you loved was in a similar situation, what would you hope they would do? What would you encourage them to do or think about if they asked for your feedback?

6) Has there been any progression in the issue toward betterment? Or does it stay the same (stagnant), or has it slowly gotten worse (decompensating)?

7) How often in this situation do you find yourself happy? Satisfied? Content? What about frustrated? Irritated? Discontent?

8) Has anyone in your life noticed the issue? What concerns have they raised, if any? Are they the type of people whose perspective you can trust?

9) How much of your time is spent managing this situation? This may even be time managing your own emotional responses, exhaustion, etc.

10) Take the time to make a full pros-and-cons list. Work on it over more than a day, adding as you think of things and asking people you trust to contribute to it. What do you notice once it's complete?

Considering Treatment

The first step of treatment is deciding it's worth a try. Seriously, it's up to you and no one else. If everything else we've talked about resonates as making sense and connects to what you're going through you might decide to pursue some more support. The clinical model often used to determine if someone is considering treatment is called the *transtheoretical model of change* (sorry, I didn't come up with the term, I know it's clunky). If we are invoking the transtheoretical model of change, we are talking about the "contemplation" step. It's not a commitment to anything. But it is a real chance to unpack how your use or behavior is impacting your life and the other goals you have for yourself. Oh, the questions! But hey, assuming that you are in treatment already and are happy about it or that you definitely want to consider treatment isn't fair. That's up to you, not me.

Here are some questions to help you better decide what makes sense for you. And if you decide "Okay, giving this a shot," you can share this information with your treatment provider or team. Smart clinicians will use your answers to help you develop a recovery plan and strategies that work best for you.

- What led you to start treatment if you have already? It's okay if it wasn't voluntary, honesty is important!

- What is going on in your life that you are most concerned with right now?

- What about getting professional help with these issues worries you? (Like, maybe that you won't be believed or understood. Or you will be pushed to do something you don't want to do. Stuff like that).

- How would you like your life to be different in the future?

- How might treatment support that process, if all goes well?

- What about you demonstrates your capacity to create that life you want for your future self?

- What are some signs that this treatment partnership is supporting you doing this work/getting yourself there?

- Most people don't engage in any behavior in a problematic or addictive way from the get-go. Maybe you used something for acute pain (physical or emotional). Or to relax. Or to have fun. What initially got you interested? What do you enjoy about it?

- Some people find that if they continue with this use or behavior, the nature of those reasons changes or their amount of use changes. Have you experienced any changes in how/when/why you use from when you first started? If yes, how so?

- Some people are able to engage in a lot of behaviors or substance use with seemingly no ill effects on the rest of their lives. They still make it to work or school. They don't appear to have any family problems. And maybe you fall into this category. If that is the case, have you noticed any small changes in your functioning? Maybe stuff no one else has even noticed but you are aware of. Also, do you think that not using or engaging in these behaviors may increase your functioning any? In measurable (time, money, sleep) or immeasurable ways (energy, stress)? How so?

- Have your usage or behaviors influenced your thoughts, feelings, or judgements in any way? How so? Have you noticed that you only act in certain ways when using/engaging in this particular behavior? What is different? What outcomes have those differences caused?

- If you stopped using/engaging in a particular behavior what would you miss most? What else would need to change in your life to make it possible? What would you gain? What new things would be possible? Is the trade-off worth it?

Harm Reduction

You know. The getting-better part. Whether it be an addiction or an out of control behavior, we're all here hoping to get better, right? But then all the acronyms, and options, and expense—you want to know more about what is really out there, right? First of all, there are two big treatment categories: abstinence and harm reduction.

Abstinence means you no longer do the thing. Like, at all. Which is considered the gold-standard of care for true addictions, though it isn't always a tenable solution. The other is harm-reduction. Harm reduction makes far more sense for most out of control behaviors because we are finding ways to be back in control. Because nothing that falls under the out-of-control-behavior category can be entirely avoided. Well, sex and porn I guess? But that tends to not work out super well for people.

Harm-reduction has been around since the 1980s, and I saw it finally embraced by community mental health by the aughts. Even for incredibly dangerous addictions (opioid addiction, for the record, is the mental health diagnosis that kills more people than any other). But it isn't always a realistic goal. Anything that reduces mortality and morbidity is considered harm-reduction—such as needle-exchange programs for opioid addiction. Or within my own work in the field, I have found that harm reduction often leads to abstinence because it creates some space for healing and clarity.

General Guidelines for Overall Safer Use

While the SMART goal setting tool later in this book is useful for both reducing use or quitting altogether, this section is more about reducing *harm* around use (something we don't talk about near enough). Whether you're reading for yourself, a loved one, or you're a professional in the field, please don't skip this section . . . you may be in a position where these pragmatics save someone's life . . . and we can't get to recovery otherwise.

Do keep in mind that most of the resources are designed for readers in the US. You may live somewhere with much better access to these items or somewhere much worse.

- Make sure you eat and drink something before use. If you have snacks and water around for after use, you are also increasing your chances of remembering to stay hydrated and care for your body's nutritional needs.

- Make sure to rest. If you can sleep, do so. If you are too wired to sleep, at least rest your body. Seriously, though. Many of the people who didn't need immediate hospitalization for overdose ended up there later with hallucinations or aggressive behavior because they had no sleep on top of their use.

- Prepare for as many other safety needs around overdose, contamination, and infection based on your other needs (as discussed in more detail in the following sections).

Lessen Chances of Overdose

- Don't be alone. It is always safer to have someone with you that you trust—90 percent of opioid overdoses occurred when the person using was alone. Make a use plan with that person, discussing what you are and are not comfortable with. Talk to them about the other harm-reduction supplies you have on hand (more on these specifics throughout this section). If you aren't at home, plan for a safe way to get home (don't drive yourself if you're under the influence!). If you live in an area that has a safe-use center, consider going there. If that is not available, please consider using the Lifeguard app or a similar product if you can get access. You set it up ahead of time with your phone number, which allows you to be geolocated. You enter the drug you are using, and it sets a timer to check on you. If you aren't able to respond, emergency services are deployed to your location.

- Don't presume your tolerance either based on the tolerance of people around you or on your previous tolerance if you haven't used in awhile.

- Start with a lower, slower dose. You can build up if you feel you need more. If you are using a new substance or you haven't used in awhile, use a slower method of use. Swallowing instead of injecting or inhaling, for example.

- Recognize signs of overdose. That way you can call emergency services for help if you notice the signs in yourself and anyone else around you who is also using. Things like headaches, chest pain, seizures, delirium, agitation/anxiety, and problems breathing require emergency care.

- Get a naloxone kit and learn how to use it. Even if just from online articles and videos. Naloxone reverses an opioid overdose (heroin, fentanyl, codeine, etc.). Even if you think you are not taking an opioid, many other drugs are being cut with fentanyl, which is a synthetic opioid that is cheap to make and is 50 to 100 times more potent than morphine. Fentanyl has been found in cocaine, ketamine, methamphetamines, and other drugs tested across the US. Public health officials attribute fentanyl to the rise in drug-related deaths during a time period where drug use is decreasing, and many states are increasing access to naloxone for just this reason. Read your state's access rules and find valuable resources about naloxone, including information about third party prescribing and standard prescription orders here: safeproject.us/naloxone/awareness-project/state-rules

- Test your substances for fentanyl. Many states are moving to remove fentanyl test strips from their lists of illegal drug paraphernalia. You can search to see if they are available in your state; many harm-reduction programs will provide them for free upon request. If you don't have them available in your area or you just want to purchase your own discreetly, they are only about a dollar a test strip. Keep in mind that the strips only indicate if fentanyl is present, not how much is present. Websites that provide test strips include:
  dancesafe.org/shop
  dosetest.com/product/fentanyl-test-strips
  bunkpolice.com/product/fentkit

- Don't mix substances. You could end up with a potentially dangerous interaction. This includes using alcohol and drugs together or drugs and prescription medications. Some common high-risk combos include benzodiazepines mixed with other depressants like alcohol, opioids, and GHB. Any depressant drugs shouldn't be mixed in general, as the effects of the combination on the central nervous system can impede brain function and halt your breathing. MDMA shouldn't be mixed with antidepressants (because the combo can cause serotonin syndrome) or any other drug that changes heart rate or blood pressure (meth, cocaine, and all sedatives). A great resource on cautions around mixing drugs, alcohol, and medications is: drugcocktails.ca

Preventing Infection, Cross-Contamination, STIs, Pregnancy, and Other Unintended Consequences

- Use new equipment every time. Most larger cities now have needle exchange programs, which can make a huge difference in transmitting infections such as HIV and hepatitis. Clean supplies can also help lessen the chance of spreading other bacteria that could be on the cooker, in the water, etc. The following website maintains a database of sites across the US that offer needles, gloves, and other supplies. Many of these agencies also offer medical care, should that be a current need. nasen.org

- You can also order supplies from this harm reduction site: nextdistro.org

- Along with using clean supplies, wash your hands and use an alcohol pad to wipe down your skin before injecting. It's also important to rotate your injection sites and take care of your skin where it has been pierced, giving it time to heal.

- Don't skin pop instead! Skin popping (injecting under your skin instead of into a vein) leads to a high chance of developing an abscess.

- If you inject your drugs through your anal cavity (booty bumping or boofing), it is far less damaging to your body to mix your drugs with water first and insert them with a clean syringe (NEEDLE REMOVED) or a lube injector with a little bit of lubricant on the tip. Lie on your side and keep hold of the end of the injector so it doesn't get lost up in there.

- If you smoke crack cocaine, wrap the end of your pipe with tape or use a rubber holder so you don't burn your lips. Additionally, use steel wool as a filer or a wire screen so you don't accidentally inhale hot particles. And let the pipe cook down between hits.

- If you snort, don't share straws (or rolled up paper or whatever) since this is another way to transmit infections.

- If you like to have sex when using, prepare ahead of time as much as possible. If you are capable of getting pregnant, consider going on a longer-term form of birth control that doesn't require daily pills (like an IUD or a Levonorgestrel-releasing implant).

- You can also reduce the risk of pregnancy and STIs by using barrier methods such as external and internal condoms, dams, gloves, and lubricant, and you can get those from state and municipal health departments, family planning clinics, colleges and universities, some high schools, and other prevention-based agencies. Two places to help you either find these items that you can pick up locally or have mailed to you are: condomfinder.org goodrx.com/health-topic/sexual-health/free-condoms

  Do make sure that if you are using lubricant with your silicone barrier method that it isn't oil-based. And if you don't have a sex dam available, plastic wrap works just fine (though it does NOT work as a condom).

- Also consider getting on pre-exposure prophylaxis (PrEP), which is very effective in preventing HIV. If you are not on PrEP and have an exposure, you can also look into getting post-exposure prophylaxis (PEP), which is a 28-day prescription treatment that you must start as soon as possible and within a 72-hour window of exposure. Many community clinics and HIV prevention programs provide both PrEP (as a pill or injectable) and PEP at no charge. You can also utilize the Health and Human Services program in the US to pay for the medication by getting the prescription written by any provider by enrolling at: readysetprep.hiv.gov or calling (855) 447-8410

- If you end up having unprotected sex and can get pregnant, you can take a morning-after contraception pill (often referred to as Plan B). Like PEP, morning-after contraception needs to be taken as soon as possible and within 72 hours after having sex. Morning-after pills can be found at most pharmacies and superstores that have a family planning section. They are also on websites such as Amazon and cost about ten dollars. You may be able to access it from your local community health clinic or family planning clinic. Do keep in mind that if you weigh over 165 pounds, the brand Ella will be more effective.

- If you do find out you are pregnant and don't want to be, if it is still under ten weeks you may be able to access a medication abortion. Information on doing so (including information on accessing the medication in states that have banned it can be found at): plancpills.org/find-pills

- If it is past the ten-week window and you live in state that has made abortion illegal, information on finding a safe and legal abortion elsewhere can be found here: abortionfinder.org/abortion-guides-by-state

Treatment Programs

Inpatient/Residential Rehab

Inpatient care just means care received in a hospital or facility that you stay at all day and all night during treatment. It is designed to pull you out of the life that was supporting use so you can focus solely on recovery without being surrounded by temptation. Sometimes it is a huge relief to have all choice taken away from you for a period of time so you can build up the skills you need to make different ones in the future.

PHPs and IOPs

A Partial Hospital Program (PHP) or Intensive Outpatient Program (IOP) are other treatment options available. Both of them require spending a good amount of time each week receiving care that involves group therapy, individual therapy, medication management, and case management. PHP programs are somewhat more intensive than IOPs in that you go in every day for four to eight hours a day, and IOPs are generally only three days a week and only for a few hours each day instead of most of the day. PHPs are designed to be a step down from inpatient/residential treatment, still allowing you to go home in the evenings, and IOPs tend to be one more step down from PHPs.

Both allow a level of re-engagement with everyday life, meaning you get your evenings and weekends like a regular human, but you have a high level of treatment and support during the day, allowing an easier transition back into everyday life in recovery.

I've worked at more than one PHP/IOP program in my years in community mental health, running both traditional therapy groups and specialty groups like an addictions group or a dialectical behavioral therapy group. They are a huge commitment and a ton of effort to participate in, but I have seen both make enormous differences in people's lives.

Outpatient Care

Outpatient care is what I do now. And what a lot of treatment providers and clinicians do now. This means seeing your prescriber every few months and/or your therapist every week or so to continue treatment and maintain support. It also may include medical care, nutritional support, neurofeedback, therapy groups, and anything else that supports your recovery. Anything where you make an appointment, go to the appointment, then go on with the rest of your day.

Peer Support

I grew up within the framework of AA: Alcoholics Anonymous. My father was in recovery, so we spent enormous amounts of time at AA meetings, events, conferences, and having our house full of people new in their sobriety. AA was unique when it was created some eighty years ago. The idea is people with lived experience sharing their support and helping others on the path to finding their own sobriety. It's based on giving yourself over to a higher power, whatever that happens to be for you. Many people who struggle with faith-based services are uncomfortable with this framework. And other prescriptive elements have emerged in some groups that feel exclusionary. For instance, many groups believe that sobriety means no mind-altering substances, even medications for a mental health disorder.

It's a shame because the AA model can also be of great benefit to healing. Higher Power? For some people that may just be the greater community surrounding you. Healthy relationships, attunement to your own authentic voice. It doesn't have to be an omnipotent God of some form. And you shouldn't have to give up the medications that are keeping you sane while letting go of the addictions that sent you on the road to crazy.

And there are plenty of groups that do honor those differences in beliefs, whether it be AA, NA, GA, DDA, or any other twelve-step model program. There are meetings available online twenty-four hours a day, and in most communities throughout the world. There are meetings that focus on special groups of individuals who may not be comfortable in general meetings, such as Lambda AA, which was created for LGBTQ individuals in recovery and the Wellbriety movement, which focuses on the specific needs of Indigenous individuals (but is inclusive for anyone to join).

There are other plans outside the traditional twelve-step model that are also abstinence-based, such as Self-Management Recovery and Training (SMART) Recovery, Save Our Selves/Secular Organizations for Sobriety (SOS), Women for Sobriety, Moderation Management (harm-reduction based!), and LifeRing Secular Recovery. These programs have also been around for some time but focus on newer research about making sobriety effective. They generally also have more of a focus on self-efficacy/internal locus of control rather than relationality/higher power support.

That's a simplification, but my point is that there are sober living options outside of the twelve-step model, a list of some of the best known ones is available at the end of this book. And a variety of options mean a larger chance of finding something that makes sense for you.

Another peer support option is with recovery coaches. Slightly more formal than going to a meeting and finding a sponsor, recovery coaches often work within community mental health systems and other community recovery programs. They are people who also have lived experience with a substance use disorder and are there to help support your recovery and assist with your access to care, kind of like a patient navigator in a hospital or a family partner who works with parents who have a child in the mental health care system. The requirements for recovery coaches are determined by each state in the US, which includes the required training and testing necessary to be certified. And unlike other coaching programs, where certification is determined by an outside governing body, recovery coach certification is generally managed by the state itself, as they do with clinical licensure.

Types of Treatment Providers

I have people ask me quite often for a referral for one type of practitioner, and it becomes clear when talking to them that they know what they need but not who provides it. This is especially the case when it comes to addiction treatment since we have even more layers of options. So please consider this a very brief and super vague breakdown of possible providers. I'm sure I'm missing people. You can @ me about it if you feel it's important. The official names for certain types of providers vary from state to state. So what is referred to as an LPC in many places may be referred to as a LMHC in other places. Just to keep you on your toes and keep everything a little bit spicy.

Psychiatrist/Medical Doctor/Doctor of Osteopathic Medicine/Physician's Assistant/Nurse Practitioner/Other Sundry Prescribers

Prescriber is the important word here. Psychiatrists are MDs, they prescribe medications more than anything else. Psychiatric nurse practitioners (NPs) also specialize in mental-health prescribing and work with a supervising physician even if they are in private practice. Both psychiatrists and psychiatric NPs do have some talk therapy training and may employ it, but that's generally not their focus. And they generally aren't doing hour-long sessions. If you are needing medications as part of your recovery process, though, they are your people. Additionally, there are other prescribers (family practice docs for example) that will support addiction recovery to their level of training and comfort. If your medication needs are relatively simple, your regular doctor may be utterly fine with prescribing and following-up with you on this care. If you live out in the sticks, this may be your best or only option, which is one of the reasons why the US government recently loosened restrictions on prescribing Suboxone.

Licensed Psychologist

A psychologist generally focuses on assessment and diagnosis more than talk therapy. Again this is a big generalization and may not be true in your case, but clinical psych programs do skew in that direction. While any licensed clinician can complete an assessment and offer a diagnostic impression or an informed opinion on someone's mental health (within the scope of their particular license, state laws regarding that license, and further trainings as necessary, especially around psychological testing), the idea is that this was the speciality domain of psychologists. If you are wanting a comprehensive assessment done (in the vein of *something* and maybe more than one something-is-wrong-and-can-you-please-figure-it-out), it will quite likely be a psychologist who does it. Out in the community, psychologists are doctoral-level clinicians (PhD or PsyD), where in the school system a school psychologist has a master's in school psychology or educational psychology, and their scope of practice is specific to the assessment and treatment planning youth need in order to be successful in the school environment.

Licensed Professional Counselor (LPC)

There are a few different terms out there because YMMV by state, but licensed professional counselors, licensed mental health counselors, etc. are historically focused on being wellness-based, offering talk therapy and other clinical support for individuals with mental health/emotional health needs. When we talk about seeing a therapist, this is generally the group of people we are talking about seeing. The "terminal degree" (which means the highest available degree in the field) is a master's degree, though you will find professional counselors with PhDs and PsyDs as well. My PhD is in counselor education and supervision, a research and teaching degree developed around teaching other people how to be professional counselors and doing research that elevates the profession. There are also a lot of individuals who got a doctoral degree in psychology but kept an LPC license, which is somewhat easier to complete than what is required for a licensed clinical psychologist. And schools are starting to offer PhDs in professional counseling, very slowly increasing the options within the profession. No matter what degree, the standards are still rigorous. LPCs have years of graduate school including internships where they provide counseling services, exit exams, more exams from the state for licensure, and required supervision of a trained clinical supervisor for their first several thousand hours of practice before they are allowed to make their own decisions. That being said, they may not have (much) experience or training in your particular area and aren't necessarily the best fit for you, and you may need to sift through who is available to find your person (see the section on, hopefully, finding a therapist that can actually help you in a system that has made that really hard to do). You will also find individuals with specialized licensure or certification around music, art, sex, nutrition, somatics, and other healing modalities.

Licensed Marriage and Family Therapist (LMFT)

LMFTs are very similar to LPCs in terms of training and licensure requirements. The big difference is an LMFT training program focuses on working with couples and families. Which means the nomenclature around the license actually matches the intent, so yaaaay! The primary difference is their master's programs have more training on working with relationships, and they are required to have a certain number of their internship hours working with couples and/or families. Like LPCs, a doctorate isn't required for independent licensure, but you will see practitioners who have a PhD, which will focus more on research and teaching or a DMFT, which is a specialized clinically-focused doctorate.

Licensed Social Worker (LMSW/LCSW)

I know, right? So many different options, no wonder everyone is confused! Licensed social workers have more training on macro needs. Meaning, their masters programs look at systems of care, not just the care of individuals. They also have more training around coordinating services for their clients. So not just "talking to people" but "helping people access things they need." Licensure is managed differently state to state, but generally you can become licensed upon graduation and state exam, and with more supervised hours aimed toward individual therapy you can become a "clinical" social worker and can have an independent, private practice.

Master Addiction Counselor (MAC)

A Master Addiction Counselor is a voluntary certification that is available to masters and doctoral level licensed clinicians with extra training and clinical hours working with individuals with substance abuse issues (five hundred contact hours in addictions training and six thousand supervised hours [which is twice what the state of Texas requires for full licensure of an LPC . . . your license and state miles may vary], plus a whole other national exam). You won't see a lot of MACs in your search for treatment providers because of these prerequisites, which aren't unreasonable but sometimes hard to access depending on where you train. It is also more to keep up with, and all extra licenses and certifications cost money. I've been MAC-qualified for over a decade but have never applied for it (much to the frustration of some of my doctoral program professors). I've only ever had one individual ask me about it and was impressed enough that I was qualified for my MAC that they didn't care that I never tested for it. So if you find a MAC to work with, you quite likely found a badass who is really committed to recovery work.

Licensed Chemical Dependency Counselor (LCDC)

Requirements to be an LCDC vary state to state but are generally a less restrictive entry point into the profession.

Some states require a bachelor's degree and others only an associates degree. In many places, an individual with a high school diploma or equivalency can engage in a specific amount of contact hour training (in Texas it's 270 hours). This training still focuses on counseling theory, ethics, and all the clinical basics with a focus on addiction science. LCDCs are also still required to complete internships, take a state exam, and complete thousands more clinical hours under supervision. Their work in the field is limited, by degree and training, to substance-use work. Many people who are LCDCs have lived experience with addiction and recovery, though it isn't a requirement of the licensure.

Certified Recovery Coach

Peer professionals are becoming increasingly common in the mental health field and certified recovery coaches are one of these groups. These are individuals who have lived experience with addiction and recovery (unlike the licensed positions that do not) and they provide nonclinical support in supporting the recovery of others. They are subject to training and supervision and testing as laid out by the state (versus other coaching-type programs, like life coaching, that do not have state oversight), though the requirements are going to be less than that of a licensed individual since the role is peer support not clinical support.

Sponsor

Unlike a recovery coach, a sponsor has no training or oversight for their role, and is someone who operates as a mentor or guide to others going through recovery as someone who has gained experience in recovery. Sponsors are generally tied to one particular peer fellowship program (like AA), and they help new individuals navigate membership within that program and assist them in working through the program.

Case Manager

A case manager is typically an individual with a bachelor's degree and prescribed training in mental health and community support. If a case manager is working for a state-funded agency there are certain educational and training standards associated with their profession (in Texas you become certified as a Qualified Mental Health Professional, for example), though if the program you are interested in is funded by different means, any affiliated case managers may have different training and experience. Case managers are your go-to people for accessing resources. Whether that be finding you a detox program, bus tickets to get to a meeting, or help with your electric bill because sitting in the dark isn't great for any aspects of your health.

Why Can't I Find a Fucking Therapist?????

I get emails on the regular from people asking if they can see me. Or do I know someone in the state they're in? Or how should someone go about searching for a therapist?

Y'all, it sucks. I know. It already sucked and was shitty before Covid-19. Now it seems nearly fucking impossible. Because it is.

Therapists are also overfull and burned out and processing the same trauma at the same time. The good ones are aware of their limits and are limiting their schedules, wait lists, and new client onboarding.

I generally start with recommending *Psychology Today* as a place to search for providers in your area not because this is a #sponcon post, but if a therapist is advertising, this is the site that is used the most (though therapist.com is gunning for a takeover). And it lets you search by speciality, location, and the like. And lets you exclude certain types of therapists as well.

But what if you STILL can't find anyone? You can't get any return calls for anybody? Then what?

When we're in a scarcity-based system, it really becomes about self-advocacy and personal connections. Yes, I understand that no healthcare should require this level of hustle. You don't need to @ me, it's already a hard agree. But it's also reality.

And while this isn't a plea for congress to write off student loan debt in exchange for providing services to underserved individuals, THAT WOULD FIX A LOT OF THINGS FOR EVERYONE.

This is about how to advocate for your own treatment needs, and I can help you with that part.

1) Most clinicians do have a few available time slots even if their schedule is closed. We save them for client emergencies and the like. Ask your friends, family, and other treatment providers who they think is great and ask them to help you get an appointment if they can (which is just "my friend so-and-so needs to see someone, can I have her email you?"). Then, when you follow up, drop the name of the person who referred you. "Hi Faith! My friend Nancy said you may be able to get me in if my schedule is flexible!" is plenty for me to remember true connection. Even if the clinician in question is completely full, we may be able to give you a solid referral to someone we know and trust. I give referrals locally to people I have trained and/or trust and will ask the clinician in question to please follow up with the individual I'm sending their way. It's not a warm-handoff but is the closest thing to one. I just got a new prescriber referral through a friend who got it from a social media group. Sometimes we gotta dig for a while. Sucks, but not getting care sucks more.

2) Check in with your local rape crisis center. If your trauma history involves sexual assault, they will likely have no-fee care available for you. But if they don't or if your trauma work is not related to sexual abuse or assault, they will still quite likely have a list of trauma-informed clinicians that they refer to.

Then you can say you were referred by them, which can also help you get in the door.

3) Same goes with any LGBTQ-pride centers in your area. Or progressive organizations like Planned Parenthood. They will quite likely have lists of affirming providers. Awesome if you need a letter for gender confirmation treatment, but also awesome if that's not your issue but knowing the provider is a trusted entity is still useful. And then you can say that's the organization that referred you. And if you *are* needing affirming and competent care and the clinician in question is full, they'll be able to point you in the right direction. I've had associates provide the needed assessment, and I co-signed on their behalf (especially helpful if a doctoral-level clinician was requested by the insurance company or surgeon's office or whatever).

4) The online platforms? There are some great clinicians who use them because they make life so much easier for their practice management. You might find a good fit. And since it's a subscription service, if you don't like your therapist or any of the others that you try out after requesting a switch, you can just cancel. My hesitation isn't about the quality of the clinician but the apps themselves. Do look at their privacy policies and what data they share by doing an online search. Also check them for BBB complaints.

Many have gotten popped for being shady in how they share data (these are tech companies after all), and your choice of platform may be determined on privacy policies.

5) Check with the local colleges that train clinicians, schools that have master and doctoral clinical programs. This is also helpful if you're broke AF and are looking for free or inexpensive-as-possible care. Most schools have an onsite clinic or have an agreement with clinics in the area where you can see a student counselor who is being highly supervised by a professor or other elder statesman of the field. Bonus? Sometimes specialty care may be available for free if a student is working on their thesis or dissertation or a professor is conducting some clinic research. I've helped people get free neurofeedback that way, as an example.

Okay, cool. Now how do you ascertain if they are a **good** clinician for your particular issue? It can be hard to suss out if it's going to be a good personality match for you. Which is a nice way of saying there are plenty of great clinicians that may not be great for you. There are always people who don't like my style, my approach, or my tattoos. And that's utterly fine. Seriously, the meta-analytic studies (see Bruce Wampold's book *The Great Psychotherapy Debate* if you are intrigued) of different therapeutic techniques show that when it comes down to it, the common factors are the most important. Common factors is just an academic way of saying the relationship building and maintenance of therapy. Meaning y'all work well together and you trust your clinician and y'all's process. And that may not be something you can guess by reading their website.

That being said? It is utterly okay to ask them about their training and experience around certain topics. There are plenty of therapists out there who market themselves as affirming but say microaggressive bullshit on the regular. Or say they are trauma-informed but are really just trauma-aware. Please (no, seriously, PLEASE) ask that question if it's important to you. If they are offended by the question this isn't going to be a good experience for you, I promise. Ask "What is your experience and training around working with non-cis folx?" or "I am seeking an assessment and diagnosis (if appropriate) of autism . . . is that something you provide?" or "How do you approach trauma work?" or even just "Do you work with couples? I'm seeking an appointment for myself and my partner." None of these questions require super long and intensive answers, and they are entirely reasonable.

And if you're a politician who wants to advocate for more student loan write-offs? Holler at your girl, I have ideas.

Detox

The idea of helping people rid their body of the effects of a drug isn't as old as you'd think it is. In 1958, the American Medical Association declared alcoholism a disease, which paved the way for recognizing that individuals struggling with a substance use disorder needed some fucking care. Detoxification, however, started being considered substance abuse treatment—and it is not. It can be part of the continuum of care, but it is intended to help a person through the dangerous part of substance withdrawal, thus allowing them the opportunity for substance abuse treatment. Detox is designed to help us evaluate, stabilize, and provide entry into treatment upon completion, should treatment be desired.

Some substances require a medical detox (alcohol and heroin being the two big ones) to prevent serious medical complications or even death. Of course, some substances are just a bitch to detox, even if they don't involve medical risk. Anyone who is a caffeine addict? You know how bad it feels when you don't get your fix. Refried ass is an apt term.

The Substance Abuse and Mental Health Services Administration operationalizes the purpose of detox thusly:

Detoxification is a set of interventions aimed at managing acute intoxication and withdrawal. Supervised detoxification may prevent potentially life threatening complications that might appear if the patient were left untreated. At the same time, detoxification is a form of palliative care (reducing the intensity of a disorder) for those who want to become abstinent or who must observe mandatory abstinence as a result of hospitalization or legal involvement. Finally, for some patients it represents a point of first contact with the treatment system and the first step to recovery. Treatment/rehabilitation, on the other hand, involves a constellation of ongoing therapeutic services ultimately intended to promote recovery for substance abuse patients.

Detox means monitoring for dangerous symptoms, administering medication as needed to manage both dangerous and uncomfortable symptoms,[12] managing other medical needs (blood sugar stabilization, etc.), making sure that the individual is getting healthy foods and staying hydrated, able to sleep, etc. It's about keeping the body as healthy as possible while the body does its job of ridding itself of the poison.

Know Your Meds

Raw dogging reality on a good day is hard enough. If you are in recovery from a substance use disorder or are struggling with an out of control behavior, you definitely need some fucking support in your life. And support can (and quite often SHOULD) include medications. Here is the best of what we know about medications that assist recovery. Medications can include help with withdrawal symptoms and with psychological cravings (whether a true addiction or an out of control behavior). Medications can also help treat the underlying conditions that have allowed the problem behavior to flourish.

In the US, the Food and Drug Administration (FDA) has domain over medication approval, and the Drug Enforcement Administration (DEA) determines the classification of the

---

12 My favorite herbalism professor supported my caffeine detox a few years ago with adaptogenic herbs. I reduced use far faster and with almost no headaches cuz she's brilliant.

medication (there are five total) based on what the drug is appropriately used for and what its potential for misuse is. This can assist with safe use but also be a barrier to treatment access, which we will discuss as we discuss particular medications.

Methadone

First approved by the FDA in 1947 for analgesic and antitussive uses, methadone hydrochloride has been the primary medication used to treat opioid addiction. It was shown to be an effective treatment in the late sixties, and FDA approval was expanded for this use in 1972. Meaning, as old as I am, methadone as a treatment for opioid addiction is a wee bit older.

Methadone has been classified as a "weak-acting opiate," meaning it acts similarly to an opioid such as heroin but without the euphoric high; therefore, it decreases the symptoms of opiate withdrawal.

Since it has been around so long, we have over three decades of research around its use and have found the following benefits when prescribed at an appropriate dose: reduced use of all illicit drugs (not just opiates), reduction in crime, reduced risk of contracting HIV, and general improvement in individual functioning. So, it not only helps the individual with the substance use disorder, it also provides a measure of protection for the community that individual lives in.

Because it is a legal narcotic, methadone is still considered a controversial medication, making access difficult for many people. Methadone is subject to the general requirements that FDA requires of all prescription drugs, as well as by the DEA because of its potential for misuse. The DEA has classified methadone as a schedule II controlled substance. Methadone also has a special third tier of distribution standards, set up by the Department of Health and Human Services, which have been implemented with FDA regulations, jointly with the National Institute on Drug Abuse (NIDA) since 1980 and, since 1993, with the Substance Abuse and Mental Health Services Administration (SAMHSA), and before that with the the National Institute on Drug Abuse from 1980-1993.

It can only be dispensed with someone who has a confirmed Opioid Use Disorder diagnosis and can only be dispensed through a SAMHSA certified Opioid Treatment Program (OTP), hospital pharmacies, and physicians registered with both the FDA and DEA, and is often subject to more restrictions by many state governments, as well as county and municipal governance.

Buprenorphine

Buprenorphone is a opioid partial agonist, similar to methadone but not as strong. It was first marketed in the US in 1985 as a schedule V narcotic analgesic but was approved in 2002 for the treatment of narcotic addiction. The Department of Health and Human Services recommended that the DEA schedule it as a Schedule III drug, which they did.

Unlike naloxone (below), buprenorphine can be prescribed and/or dispensed from a physician's office. Historically, physicians can treat up to thirty individuals at a time without specialized training, with those numbers increasing after training and time spent prescribing. Hoping to increase access in rural areas, the Health Resources & Services Administration (HRSA) launched an effort in 2021 to encourage prescribers to utilize the medication by offering $3000 payments to every provider who trained to obtain the waiver necessary to treat more than a limited number of patients.[13]

But, hey! This requirement changed at the time of me writing this book. Section 1262 of the Consolidated Appropriations Act, 2023 (also known as the 2023 omnibus bill), removes the federal requirement for practitioners to submit a Notice of Intent (have a waiver) to prescribe medications like buprenorphine for the treatment of opioid use disorder (OUD). I am writing this at a time where we are actually really working to improve access to this medication, and it's a good start.

Naloxone

Naloxone reverses an opioid overdose by blocking the effects of said opioid, by restoring normal breathing within two to three minutes. Because tens of thousands of people die by opioid overdose each year, the World Health Organization

13 Without the waiver, prescribers were limited to only thirty patients at a time. After specialized training, the number goes up to one hundred for the first year, then 275 after that.

(WHO) has declared it to be an essential medication for any functioning healthcare system.

If you have a family member taking opioids, if you are on a high dose of opioids yourself (for any reason), or if you work with individuals who take opioids, carrying naloxone is highly recommended and is now available in every state . . . often with standing orders (which means that you can walk into a pharmacy and buy it) and Good Samaritan laws to protect you from prosecution for giving it to someone. Research has found that it isn't dangerous to give, so err on the side of using it versus not using it if someone shows signs of overdose. Though if you do give it to them, stay until emergency help arrives or at least four hours to make sure their breathing returns to and remains normal. Information on how to find the laws regarding getting and carrying naloxone in your state are provided in the resource section of this book.

Naltrexone

Naltrexone is an agent that blocks opioid receptors, particularly the μ-opioid receptor. Use of this agent in animal models leads to a reduction of dopamine levels in the nucleus accumbens. Meaning it takes the euphoria and relaxation out of the use, therefore reducing use. It was first synthesized in 1963 and was approved by the FDA for opioid addiction in 1984. It has since been found to also be of use for alcohol use disorders and gambling disorders (big hint: this is a huge part of why gambling addiction is the only process addiction currently listed in the DSM). It is being suggested for out of control behavior (OCB) treatment, and some case studies show that it may be effective when combined with antidepressant therapy, but there is still little data beyond these singular reports.

It can be taken as a daily pill or a monthly injection but cannot be started until substance detox is complete.

Acamprosate

Acamprosate a medication that helps sustain sobriety from alcohol. It is not a preventative and does not prevent withdrawal symptoms. It is meant to be started on day five of abstinence and reaches full effectiveness in five to eight days of use if taken three times a day. So what's the point of it? It's a neuromodulator, chemically similar to the amino acids GABA and taurine. Because alcohol abuse impacts multiple areas of the brain, many people have disrupted neurobiology which the medication is designed to assist the treatment of. Think of it as assisting the brain to be normal-er.[14]

It was first introduced in Europe in 1989 and was approved by the FDA in the US in 2004. One recent survey has found it to be the most widely prescribed medication for the treatment of alcoholism in the US. It also does not process through the liver, making it a safer option for individuals whose alcohol use has caused liver disease (or who have liver disease from any other means). Because the

---

14 Please know I'm saying "normal" with all eyerolls intended. No such thing as a normal brain. In this case, we mean "pre-alcohol-dependence brain."

medication improves attentional control in the brain, we may start seeing research demonstrating its efficacy in managing out of control behaviors.

Disulfiram

Disulfiram is the third of the three medications approved by the FDA for alcohol dependence. It is considered a second-line treatment (the above two are considered first line) and is meant to be prescribed only for patients that have good clinical supervision (meaning you go to see the doctor regularly). It is meant to be used by individuals who have already gone through detox and are newly abstinent. It is taken once a day and should not be taken within twelve hours of having used any alcohol.

Disulfiram inhibits aldehyde dehydrogenase (ALDH1A1), which is a liver enzyme used to metabolize alcohol in the body. Short version of what that does? Makes you really sick if you drink. If you take it and then try to drink, you will get hella sick in about ten minutes and remain hella suck for an hour or more. It's a medical "fuck around and find out."

Bupropion

Bupropion is marketed as an antidepressant (antidepressants are also discussed below in relation to both addictions and out of control behaviors) but also as the smoking-cessation medication Zyban. So it is showing up twice on this list. It is FDA approved for smoking cessation because it helps tamp down impulse control, helps manage cravings, and helps with withdrawal symptoms according to multiple studies.

Varenicline (Chantix)

Chantix is designed to mimic the effects of nicotine in the brain, reducing your cravings for use. It also reduces your enjoyment of nicotine somewhat because it is already attached to the nicotine receptors in the brain so the nicotine doesn't hit in the same way anymore. Chantix is designed to start using a week before your pre-determined "quit date," though some doctors will prescribe it when you don't have a planned quit date, with the hope that you will quit somewhere between day eight and thirty-five of starting the medication. Typically you are expected to take it for twelve weeks, though some prescribers will suggest going twenty-four weeks.

Antidepressants and Anxiolytics

Antidepressants are a common firstline treatment for out of control behaviors and are often a second-line treatment for use disorders (to assist in the treatment of co-occurring mental health disorders). For example, out of control sexual behavior and shopping behaviors have been shown to respond well to citalopram (Celexa), though the newer version of citalopram (escitalopram); Lexapro was found to *not* be effective for out of control shopping behaviors. Out of control tech behaviors (internet usage, gaming, etc.) displayed some benefit of escitalopram, but most benefit from bupropion (Wellbutrin). Citalopram and escitalopram also help manage anxiety, and bupropion assists somewhat with impulse control (as mentioned above).

Antidepressant efficacy is another place we can see why gambling is considered an addiction, where the other OCBs are not. Fluvoxamine (Luvox) is an antidepressant that also helps with anxiety and impulsive behaviors. It does not work on out of control shopping but does assist with gambling addiction as a secondary medication after an opioid blocker.

You'll notice this list doesn't cover any benzodiazepines (which reduce brain activity) or sedating medications. Both are more likely to be abused, therefore aren't as commonly prescribed to anyone struggling with an addiction or OCB.

Nutrition, Supplementation, and Other Complementary Support

Everything else in this chapter is pretty traditional, Western-medicine-focused treatment. But since it's me and I love my evidence-based woo-woo, let's talk about other possible treatment options. But first, let me reiterate the word *options*. The number of people who have sent me angry emails calling me a stupid cow for discussing complementary treatment options in my books is not zero.[15] And the number of emails I have gotten explaining, for example, how different antidepressants work, for example, *is* zero. Why? I imagine that since the latter category is the Western-medicine norm, it is expected that I discuss it, while the former category has limited institutional acceptance; therefore, it is seen as more sus.

---

15 Though to be fair, some of them are very very funny, and I enjoy passing them on to my publisher and editorial team.

So to be extra clear about it . . . you don't have to take Narcan *or* magnesium. You don't have to go to therapy *or* reiki. I am not forcing or even suggesting that you do anything that doesn't seem like a good or necessary idea to you. My job is to offer information on as many treatment options I have enough competence to speak to. Allowing you, in turn, to do your own lit review, chat with your treatment providers, and make decisions for yourself. Especially since, like the Western-medicine treatment options, this is a very broad overview designed to give you both (1) hope that there are more options out there than you expected and that something may resonate as a possibility, and (2) confirmation that all of this is incredibly complex; all support and care should be individualized to your specific needs.

Nutrition and Supplementation

Substance use and some out of control behaviors (particularly those around food and exercise, which have a more immediate impact on the physical body) can lead to significant wear and tear on our bodies. Nutritional deficiencies are common occurrences with substance use not just because of making less-helpful food choices but because of how the substance changes the makeup of the body. For example, one of the most common causes of nutritional deficiencies in the Western world is alcohol use. Up to 80 percent of people who have an alcohol use disorder have a vitamin B1 (thiamine) deficiency, which can cause anemia and neurological problems.[16] In this case, the ingestion of the alcohol is causing damage to the stomach and intestines, which leads to chronic inflammation, so nutritional absorption is impaired. Someone who doesn't drink or drinks little can eat the exact same things and have better absorption than someone who drinks regularly and has done so over time.

Which is all to say, nutritional support can be a life-changing part of someone's recovery. Getting lab work done, should this be possible and affordable, can give specific information on possible deficiencies (like the thiamine example) and inflammation. And while I don't have universal advice, there are certain issues that are common enough they may merit consideration for you:

1) Blood sugar stability and support. When early in recovery, managing cravings is far easier with stable blood sugar.

2) Liver support. Because so many substances process through the liver, it can be helpful to add liver support, through milk thistle and the like, both to help rid the body of lingering substances and to get the liver as healthy as possible again.

3) Gut motility support. Substances like opioids can cause gut motility issues, which is a polite way of saying you can't poop very well. This may resolve

16 Yes, this is the etiology of Wernicke-Korsakoff syndrome ("wet brain").

over time once recovery is achieved, but it can also be helped along with probiotics, prebiotics, digestive enzymes, and the like.

4) Inflammation is another common issue, which I know I talk about so very often that if you've read my other books you're tired of hearing about it. Inflammation isn't just decreasing thiamine because of the presence of alcohol. Omega 3 fatty acids can be increased through fish oil, blue green algae supplementation, or ahiflower supplementation and can help enormously. I am also a big fan of bioavailable turmeric for inflammation.

5) Dealing with anxiety and overwhelming stress is also a common concern. Especially if the substances in question were helping to medicate those same issues for some time. I'll often suggest some grounding minerals (like magnesium) and a water-extracted kava as a gentle nervous system relaxant that is non-altering at a clinical dose.

Movement

First of all, I have a confession to make.

I am absolutely one of those people who goes and works out at 5 a.m. before work. I don't do this for bragging rights, and I am not nearly a health guru for doing so. Especially since I swing by Juanitos for a breakfast taco after working out half the time. I do it because I simply feel way fucking better when I do, both physically and mentally. Honestly, it's a little irritating how much physical movement helps me in general. Chances are it will help you, too.

I don't mean grueling, punishing workouts (unless that's your kink, no shade intended), but something you enjoy. Movement should be fun. I walk laps around the park near my house in the mornings while listening to music or podcasts. I also enjoy hiking, swimming, dancing, yoga, and tai chi. Which is all to say, I do not run unless someone is chasing me with a knife. Gentle movement that you actually enjoy helps increase mindfulness of your body, which we often suppress in the face of substance use and out of control behavior engagement. That's the point, right? To medicate how we are feeling because it is shitty and overwhelming? Learning to be in your body without overwhelm is an incredibly important part of recovery. So movement gives you the physical health benefits and (I'm so sorry about how true it is) the mental health benefits.

And hey, if the idea of movement as medicine is new to you and you aren't sure what to try? There are programs specifically recovery related, yoga being a big one. Research demonstrates that doing yoga is associated with less use and fewer cravings for use in and of itself, and there are yoga programs designed specifically for recovery (like Yoga12SR).

Other Complementary Treatments

Okay, what else can be of benefit to healing the body/mind? Here I go being repetitive again about functional supports that I spent more detail on in my books *Unfuck Your Brain* and *Unfuck Your Body*. In terms of managing addictions and out of control behaviors, my go-to supports outside of nutrition and movement are neurofeedback, acupuncture, and massage. Neurofeedback can help to target all of those brain areas we discussed that help facilitate addiction and habit-creation, as well as any co-occurring mental health issues and some of the stimulus-overwhelm associated with neurodiversity. Acupuncture and massage, like mindful movement, can help you feel reconnected to your body and assist with physical issues. Both have done more for my chronic pain than any Western-medicine practice so I may be a little (lot) biased, but research does support these practices. There is a lot of blah blah blah piezoelectric fascia activation science that I've written about in *Unfuck Your Body* that shows the evidence of how it works. Which is to say there is more to it than "it feels good," though that part is nice too.

Part Three:
Defining
& Creating
Recovery

WHY RECOVERY IS SO DAMN HARD—AND YOU'RE A BADASS FOR GOING FOR IT

Before we get into some recovery skills, let's set the stage on some brain science-y stuff. This is all of the absolutely-pay-attention-to-the-man-behind-the-curtain part of recovery. Because "Just say no" is utter bullshit that has never, ever worked. And understanding the underlying issues is central to achieving and maintaining recovery. Recovery isn't just about stopping problematic behaviors. You have to understand what those "problematic" behaviors were helping you achieve. They were used to get you through something really fucking difficult. And a huge amount of your work will be figuring out what those difficult things are so you can find other ways to get through them that don't cause you the long-term harm that substances and problematic behaviors will.

Survival Mode: An Exhausted Brain Just Trying to Survive

The concept of "survival mode" is one that clinicians use a lot, though is not an official, DSM-y linguistic choice. Like the term "flashbacks," which comes from the movie practice of telling stories about a character's past, survival mode is also a media-related term that we adapted to other uses. In video games, survival mode is when we have to continue playing without dying in a pause-free game for as long as we can while the game itself gets more difficult, faster, and harder to manage. Also, no additional support is provided in the process.

So let's talk about what clinicians mean when we say someone is living in survival mode. Short version is life has been so exhausting and so overwhelming for so long their focus is on surviving, not thriving. It can be related to trauma but also stress, grief, or any other sustained difficult emotion or situation. People living in poverty (and I mean POOR, not temporarily BROKE) often live in survival mode. It means we are existing moment to moment and struggle to consider anything beyond the short term.

What's going on in survival mode? Our prefrontal cortex, the most evolved part of the human brain, is the thinking brain. It's where our executive function skills reside. Things like thinking for and planning for the future, thinking through options critically, being able to organize, and problem solve. To be able to best manage our emotions without getting the fallout from them. When we are our best selves, we are able to deliberate, consider, weigh options, and make choices grounded in all possible considerations.

I've written (ad nauseam, sorry) about how trauma affects the prefrontal cortex (in my book *Unfuck Your Brain* and every other book that has my name on it for time eternal). The term trigger, clinically, refers to the experience of reliving one's trauma of a past experience in the present. You're walking through the store, for example, and someone in there sounds just like your abusive father and suddenly you're eight years old again, ducking for cover. Your amygdala takes over.

Why? Because those older parts of the brain are not only designed for protection over reason, they work faster than the prefrontal cortex. Executive function skills require time, consideration, and discernment. And if your brain gets activated to danger, it's going to go into protective mode. We do not have time for the slower process of consideration. Staying alive means erring on the side of caution, every time.

So when clinicians are referring to survival mode, we are looking at very similar processes. We don't mean someone who is currently triggered or re-experiencing an unhealed trauma. Rather, someone who has struggled for so long to just make it through life that their executive function processes have become dimmed by the sheer volume of awful things they have to manage, the utter lack of support and care, and the paucity of healthy choices and resources. Where someone with PTSD may be triggered and react in a way for immediate escape, someone living in survival mode may be able to be somewhat future focused, but not in the long term. Their decision-making processes have become so worn thin that what may be clear to everyone around them isn't at all discernable in their current state. Think of trauma reactivity turning off the prefrontal cortex completely and survival mode as a prefrontal cortex dimmer switch.

Survival mode can look like the following:

Fatigue/Low energy: This means feeling depleted even if you get a good amount of rest (and even more fun if you haven't), and the depletion may be physical, emotional, or even spiritual.

Depleted Self-Care: Less or no self-care, either intentional ("I don't have time or space for this") or unintentional (simply forgetting). It means not eating foods that are healthy and nourishing (or eating on the run or not eating at all), not taking care of our hygiene, not maintaining a sleep schedule, not moving our bodies some.

Being Present or Near-Future Focused Only: This means we are only handling the day to day, maybe a few days out but not much past that. If we keep our heads down to stay in the grind, there isn't much time to look at what might be possible a year out if we start working toward it now.

Emotional Lability: Meaning, feeling angry, overwhelmed, sad, or other emotions far more easily than we have in the past. Which can lead to feeling activated or breaking down far more frequently.

Isolation: This could be because we are operating on autopilot and not even thinking about connecting with others. It could also be because of the exhaustion or our concern over our emotional lability. The isolation can be conscious or unconscious.

More Impulsive: This can be related to being more shortsighted, but can also exist on its own. Even if you recognize the longer-term consequences, the need to feel better in the moment takes precedence. You may use more substances, spend more money, and/or engage in activities that don't serve you well, or engage in activities to excess.

Why am I discussing this in the context of a book about addiction and out of control behavior? Well, first of all, it's far more fun to do interesting things with my books that maybe aren't expected. No one picks up a book on addictions and thinks they are going to get a mini-class on sluggish executive function. But it is incredibly relevant to both understanding and healing. The Covid-19 pandemic became a "perfect" way to study what it means to live in survival mode. When experiencing intense, ongoing stressors, many individuals adopt unhealthy coping mechanisms, such as problems with eating, substance abuse, and other harmful behaviors. This is evidenced by more than 50 percent of individuals having an unhealthier life now than before the Covid-19 pandemic.

Living in survival mode makes us far more susceptible to both picking up and maintaining an addiction or out of control behavior. *And living in survival mode makes it that much harder to achieve recovery.* If you know you aren't going to make rent anyway, why not spend the little money you do have on something that takes your mind off things for a while? If you suspect things are never going to get better, why even bother to try?

Most of the literature on the topic makes the standard suggestions about self-care and self-compassion and all the things that I adore but that feel veryVeryVERY overwhelming when your executive function has gotten so rusty. So instead of coming up with a whole new self-care schedule, I suggest being mindful and starting slowly.

- Of all the things survival mode may look like as mentioned above, which do you most recognize in yourself?

- Which one or two is the worst right now?

- How do these particular issues relate to the use/behavior that you are trying to eliminate or manage?

- What is one small thing you can add (not subtracting anything just adding!) that can help you minimize or mitigate the effect of that particular symptom (e.g. if sleep is the biggest problem, adding some tryptophan at night to help increase quality sleep; or if multitasking is the biggest problem, reconfiguring your workload so you can focus on one thing at a time)?

It may also be helpful to check in with someone you know and trust (whether a friend or a treatment provider) to help you without shaming you in managing some of the things that have become unmanageable (like budgeting, taking your meds regularly, and the like). They can help you find ways to think about yourself and your wellness in the longer term and help you gently find ways to move in that direction. As survival mode dissipates in your life, many of the other concerning behaviors may be extinguished. And if not, treating them will be much easier with a brain that isn't trying to just stay alive.

Traumatic Invalidation

I've written a lot (like, a lot A LOT) about trauma and why/how PTSD and other trauma responses develop sometimes but not other times. Short version is that fucked up things happen because they do. All the fucking time, right? If we are able to make some level of sense of what happened, if we have time to heal, if we have time to grieve, if we understand that we are not to blame, we slowly get better.

But so often, none of that care is available. Or, worse, we are told we are wrong about both our experiences and our responses to it. Because it isn't just about what happens to us, it's about how we make sense of it. It's about how we fit that experience within the context of our lives and the world around us. Gabor Maté refers to this experience throughout his documentary *The Wisdom of Trauma*. And Dialectical Behavior Therapy developer Marsha Linehan uses what I think is the perfect phrase to describe this experience: traumatic invalidation.

I didn't want to just rehash "because trauma" in this book, because I think it's a bit more subtle than that, and I agree with Dr. Maté that much of the roots of addiction and out of control behavior lie within how those around us respond to our pain rather than the pain itself.

Invalidation is the term we use to describe something that is erroneous or untrue. If someone says it's raining when it's bright and sunny and you point out the discrepancy between their statement and reality? You're invalidating their claim. It also refers to a deprivation or nullifcation based on the information being presented. You can invalidate someone's Booker Prize nomination because it turns out they plagiarized parts of their book, for example. So what takes it to the next level, making it a traumatic experience? Traumatic invalidation is what happens when we are disbelieved, discounted, or dismissed around an issue that is significant or important to us.

It can happen when a child tells their teacher that they are being abused at home and are accused of lying. Or when a child tells their parent that they are being bullied at school, and they are told to stop being dramatic and toughen up. It could be the child or adult who explains that they are physically ill or struggling with their emotional health, and they are told they are exaggerating, looking for attention, or making things up to get out of work. Or someone coming out as queer or not cisgender and being told they are going through a phase, complete with deadnaming and refusal to respect pronouns. Or showing they've been diagnosed with a form of neurodiversity, and the response is an eye roll that they are just making an excuse for laziness. Or when a person of color reports that someone else in their office or classroom or wherever is making racist comments, and they are told they are misinterpreting what is obviously a joke.

Traumatic invalidation is not being seen, heard, believed, and understood. It may come in the form of "No, that didn't happen," or in the form of "It wasn't that bad," or even in the form of "Okay, it happened, but you are taking this all way too seriously and you need to get over it." It comes from the people who are supposed to love us and protect us. Or at least are an authority figure in our lives.

Traumatic invalidation disrupts our ability to heal because it tells us we are invalid. That how we perceive the world and ourselves isn't correct. It violates our expectations of love, friendship, community, and care. It informs us we are excluded from experiencing support. It tells us that we are wrong to feel what we feel.

So not only do we cease to trust the world, we cease to trust ourselves. We experience shame. Confusion. Anger. Defensiveness. We self-abandon. We either become desperate for connection and care, even from dangerous places, or we isolate and disconnect. We seek ways of medicating the overwhelm of not being seen or not being worthy of care. So many addictions and out of control behaviors started as ways of coping with our perceived not-enoughness. And research demonstrates that this increases our risk of ending up with a violent partner. Of self-harming. Of suffering from PTSD and depression. Of having more physical illnesses and ailments. If humans are wired for connection and those connections are weakened or severed, it impacts our lives in enormous, far-reaching ways.

And if this resonates as part of your experience? Finding ways to validate and work through your experiences in a healthier way can be an enormously important part of recovery. Gabor Maté's aforementioned documentary shows some of that work, as it is being done in vitally important places like the prison system. Marsha Linehan includes this work as part of her interpersonal effectiveness skills training, focusing on doing some factual unpacking around the situations in question as well as some compassionate self-coaching. Here are some of the things that can help.

Fact-check the situation as clearly as possible. Self-validate whenever possible. If you need some extra perspective, you may look at sharing your experience with someone you trust to be supportive but honest. I swear, the most therapeutic thing I can say to a client sometimes is "That's fucked up, I'm so sorry."

Supportive but honest feedback may also look like, "I can see why you registered the situation that way, it absolutely makes sense to me. But I'm wondering if you saw it this way because of your personal history, and maybe what was really going on was . . . is that a possible alternative?" Validation doesn't mean you are always exactly right, it means you are allowed to feel what you feel and figure out if your feelings are congruent with the situation or if you maybe missed some pieces. Validation means you the person are valuable and loved and worthy of care, even when you have to own and correct mistakes and overreactions.

For (lots of) extra credit, start looking at the patterns surrounding these experiences for you. When your responses are outsized, and you are struggling with feeling guilty for them, remind yourself that behaviors come from somewhere. You are not stupid or wrong. You're reacting from somewhere. Where in your history may this strong response stem from? Dr. Linehan refers to this as figuring out the valid reasons for invalid behavior. So if you acted a fool over a small problem at work? Figuring out the why behind it can help enormously in changing your patterns. It's the "Ohhhhh, I see why I did that!" moment. Which leads you to come up with a better way of managing it. And hey, check out the Relapse section in this book on habit loops for some more ideas around that.

It is also important to engage in self-compassion and self-soothing when you feel disconnected and invalidated. Remind yourself that being a human is hard, and we are always growing and learning. And remind yourself that someone invalidating your experiences doesn't mean they are invalid. You are allowed to be fully human, complete with issues that you are continuing to work on. Seriously, it's an important part of your recovery work in general, not just in dealing with traumatic invalidation. One method of self-soothing with a ton of research behind it is autogenic training, discussed in the next chapter.

What Are You Hungry For?: The Five Emotional Hungers

I keep developing models of care around issues I see over and over again with my clients, family, friends, and my own dumb self. This model started as a way of figuring out what was behind using food as a self-soothing mechanism, and was published in my book *Unfuck Your Eating*. And while this book does discuss food as a potential problem behavior, I think the model works for all addictions and out of control behaviors. Because we are missing something in our lives that needs tending to. And our use drugs, alcohol, gambling, foods, sex, shopping, gaming, and all the other things we have discussed herein can often be tied to filling a hole in our lives. In short, these emotional hungers seemed relevant for a multitude of behavioral issues and addictions. So I wanted to reverse engineer my conceptualization to see if the research backed me up.

Short answer, it does. When you look closely at the research on addiction and problem behaviors it turns out, as you've seen throughout this book, that there is often underlying depression and anxiety. But also loneliness. Boredom. Stress. Traumatic stress. Worries. A construct called tense-tiredness, which I consider a level of overwhelm with which there is no hope for rest). Another big one was "confused mood" . . . meaning I feel unsettled, but I don't even know how or why. And interestingly, confused mood was expressed often by boys and men that were studied. The mechanisms by which we don't allow masculine individuals to experience and express a variety of uncomfortable emotions has led to a literal confusion about what they are feeling, resulting in reaching desperately for anything that soothes that feeling.

Which is why we often don't even enjoy whatever substance we are using or behavior we are engaging in. It becomes part of the habit loop discussed in the Relapse section but doesn't provide true healing. This model goes into the five hungers I see show up over and over in myself and the people I care about, and hope that it offers a language and a structure that can help you recognize some of the ways you've been struggling as well.

Hunger for Relief
A release from anxiety or distress. A reassurance of survival.

For example, if your partner says, "We need to talk when I get home," and you still have a few hours until they actually come home and your mind is spinning disasters? Using or engaging in less healthy behaviors can seem very appealing.

Has this hunger shown up in your life? How?

Hunger for Equanimity
A mental calmness. A brain break in the midst of chaos. A moment to regain composure. A sense of peaceful acceptance of what is, good or bad.

For example, work has been nonstop and exhausting for hours, you haven't had time to stop and think or even take a deep breath. And then, *holy shit*, there is something available that can soothe your brain for a minute.

Has this hunger shown up in your life? How?

Hunger for Control

A re-empowerment. The ability to make decisions for oneself instead of being narrated by others.

For example, you just got blessed out by your family for something that happened years ago. But there is no telling your auntie to back the fuck off for once. And using or soothing with the behavior you are trying to change is the only thing that feels like you can control right now.

Has this hunger shown up in your life? How?

Hunger for Connection

A need to be seen, heard, held, and understood. A desire for companionship and a shared experience.

For example, you've been in some level of pandemic quarantine for what seems like an endless amount of time. Or you are at school, away from all the people who have known you your whole life. You may be alone or not, but definitely lonely. And there doesn't seem to be any way to feel better than the unhealthy coping skill you are trying to keep away from.

Has this hunger shown up in your life? How?

Hunger for Meaning

A desire for purpose in the world. The ability to impact those around us for the better.

For example, you've been stuck in a job for some time that seems endless. It doesn't align with your goals and values and what you want to do in the world. You don't feel like you are where you want to be or ought to be. So you start looking for ways to alleviate the exhaustion and overwhelm of not having the life you want to live.

Has this hunger shown up in your life? How?

How to Reclaim Emotional Satiety and Equilibrium

- What situations find you reaching for ways to manage an emotional hunger?

- What clues do these situations provide about the emotional hunger (or hungers) you may be experiencing?

- What needs do you experience as unmet (if not always, at least regularly)?

- What emotional hunger best describes your situation? (*You may be completely sure or taking a stab at it. Sometimes it takes awhile to unpack and figure out what's going on inside us. If your first answer doesn't hold up to the light, just try again. That's why emotional work is always a process, and never finished.*)

- What stories are you telling yourself about what you deserve, what you are worth, or the value you have?

- What in your history led you to believe these stories about yourself?

- What fears reinforce these stories in the present?

Now picture the most accepting, kind, and loving person you can think of. Maybe someone you know, maybe a current public figure or historical figure. What would *they* say about your worth in the world? It's okay if you don't quite believe it yet. You just need to create space where it *just might possibly* be true.

- What would your accepting, kind, and loving person encourage you to do with what is currently in your control?

- What energy would that create for you?

- What would change, internally or externally?

Now focusing on your response to those questions, check in with your emotional hunger(s). What, if anything, has changed? Has anything shifted? Do you feel more satiated? Where do you feel that within your body? *(If the answer is "nothing yet" . . . keep tweaking and experimenting with these questions until something resonates within you as your truth).*

- What happened when you utilized your new response?

- What happened to your hunger?

Clear Mind Recovery

In Dialectical Behavioral Therapy (DBT), one of the goals is always to find a measure of balance in our daily lives. On the surface that may not seem to be the best way to manage an addiction or problem behavior, but if you have struggled and failed to maintain sobriety or healthy use, you have already bumped into how difficult it is to achieve the right balance. So let's look at the two extremes and the balanced middle.

Addict/Problem Mind: This is where we are actively engaging in the use or behavior that is causing us so many other life domain problems, including possible substance dependence. You are ruled or feel out of control over your engagement and your time and energy is spent on getting your "fix."

What does addict/problem mind look like? Here's some common thoughts and statements:

- Dude, this is not a problem.

- Other people have a way worse problem than I do.

- I can stop whenever. I have stopped lots in the past, which wouldn't be the case if it was a problem, see?

- Have you SEEN my life? You'd do the same to cope with this bullshit.

- Literally everyone I know does the same thing, you saying we ALL have a problem?

- I'm keeping up with (school, work, family, other obligations) just fine. So what's the worry?

What does addict/problem mind look like for you?

What are your warning signs that you are heading in that direction?

Clean Mind: This is the other extreme, where we feel so in control of not using that we aren't paying attention to triggers and warnings. We feel that we can easily avoid any temptations because we love how we feel newly clean. We're proud of our success (and should be!) but start feeling a little too invincible, because staying clean gets easier with time . . . but only if we keep using the skills that help us stay that way. If we aren't attentive, it becomes easy to relapse.

What does clean mind look like? Here are some common thoughts and statements:

- I'm totally better.

- I don't have any triggers or cues to plan around. My willpower is plenty strong.

- I'm totally cured, I don't even have to worry about this anymore.

- I can use X without using Y, even though I've used them both together in the past.

- I can go to Z place without using Y, even though I always used when I was there in the past. I don't need any support, I can do this by myself.

What does clean mind look like for you?

What are your warning signs that you are heading in that direction?

Clear Mind: This is our baby-bear middle ground. This is very similar to the DBT "wise mind." We are in recovery, in whatever form that looks like for us, while maintaining an eye on our proclivities for use and how easy it would be to fall back into use so we are using energy to keep ourselves safe.

The kinds of healthy thoughts and statements associated with Clear Mind:

- I need support to be my best self. My supports include . . .

- I need a system of accountability so I stay on track.

- I'm open to concerns and suggestions from the people who have my healthiest interests at heart.

- I'm willing to look at the underlying issues that got me to this point.

- I may not like how hard this all is, but I'm worth the effort.

What does a clear mind look like for you?

What are signs that you are maintaining a clear mind?

HELPFUL TOOLS AND PRACTICES

*T*his section contains some of my favorite recovery support tools, whether you're working with an addiction or out of control behavior. These tools aren't meant to substitute for appropriate medical and therapeutic care when indicated but to support that work. Meaning, please don't sue me if any of these skills do not create perfect sobriety for you . . . I am already a loud-mouthed progressive in Texas, which gives my lawyers enough to worry about. These are skills meant to help you determine if recovery makes sense for you, crystalize what recovery would *really* mean for you, create and sustain new and healthier habits, and unpack some of the underlying issues that helped create and sustain the struggles you are currently experiencing.

First, Where Can You Say Yes?

Addiction is often treated like a lack of willpower. Nancy Reagan[17] told us it was simple enough . . . all you have to do is just say NO.

17 For my young people who only know Nancy Regan as the throat goat? Back in the 1980s, her First Lady cause was just saying no to drugs. Like, "Meh, I'm good" instead of any real treatment or

So that becomes our internal dialogue. Why can't we, sometimes? Why can't we just say no? Which leads to a shame spiral and blocks our ability to be self-compassionate. If addictions and OCBs are replacing other relationships, that's where our first steps in healing should begin. A healthier relationship with oneself. Healthier relationships with the people you love. Hell, healthier relationships with the people you just like well enough.

And maybe you are thinking, "Did I seriously just spend money on a book telling me to replace my bad habits with good ones? Are you fucking SERIOUS with this bullshit?" Yes, that would be bullshit. And that's actually not what I'm suggesting. Instead of that, I am suggesting to do this *and* that. Meaning, we aren't looking at stopping or replacing any other behaviors at all. We are looking at adding some healthier options to the mix. Recovery isn't a zero-sum game, so let's focus not on stopping the problem stuff but adding in some of the good stuff. What happens if you take the time to eat a meal that is beautifully prepared and tastes delicious instead of eating ultra-processed snacks you picked up at the gas station? What happens if you take a walk in the evening when the weather cools down, maybe even *before* cracking open a bottle of wine?

We are going to go into strategies for making positive changes and helping yourself stick to them (the WOOP skill later in this chapter, to be precise). But for this exercise, I

---

support. It was as obnoxious and as ridiculed a platform as the Melania Trump "Be Best" campaign.

don't want you to give one single thought to replacing one thing with another or even how the healthier habit would work. Just what they might be.

What did you used to love but haven't done in a long time? What do you miss? Who do you miss? What helps you feel embodied and healthy and whole? What just sounds like fun (that doesn't involve the substance or behavior in question)? What can you say yes to? Expand the boundaries of your life back out by adding something. What happens? What shifts? What else do you need now? What do you no longer need?

The Recovery Process

Recovery is a full-on different life process. It isn't just about no longer using or engaging in problematic behavior but about creating the most healthy life possible for yourself. Just like we talked about adding good stuff back in, rather than focusing on "not using?" Same idea. Many of these tools have shown up in *How to Be Accountable*, a book I co-authored with Joe Biel. These are some of the things that I'd love for you to start thinking about in terms of your own life:

- What, exactly, do you want to change about yourself? State this in positive and behaviorally focused terms. E.g., "I want to listen to the viewpoints of others without interrupting in order to understand where they are coming from" is far more doable than "I want to stop being a judgmental asshole."

- Why do you want to change this about yourself? Why is this a personal priority?

- How will making these changes improve your life?

- How do you hope these changes will improve life for people you care about?

- How do you hope these changes will impact future relationships?

- Will anyone in your life be negatively affected by this change? Remember that any change to a system affects the whole system. Even good change can throw others into disequilibrium. If you stop drinking, others can no longer play the role of rescuing and enabling, for example. Those roles may be their way of not having to work through their own shit and they may have a negative reaction to you.

- What do you think would be a reasonable timeline to actualize this change?

- How much time will you need to set aside each week to work on making this happen? For what specific activities? How will they fit into your schedule?

- What are some harmful or painful memories or experiences from your past that you haven't yet fully resolved?

- What feedback and criticisms have other people given to you or have you heard secondhand about your behavior? Why do you think people have these opinions?

- Which of these criticisms can you accept as valid and apply to your own behavior?

- Which of these pieces of feedback about your behavior do you feel don't apply and are probably other people's stuff?

- What help do you need in making this change happen? Who can you rely upon for that help who would understand where you are coming from?

- Where can you research best practices from people who have overcome this problem in the past? Can you reach out to them directly?

- What are your best practices for moving forward? What are the actionable steps?

- What are three incidents when your intent was good but your impact was damaging?

- When you aren't too bummed out, make a list of the things that you've lost as a result of the behavior that you want to change. If you are working with a therapist, coach, sponsor, etc., getting support for this part may be of benefit to you.

- How do you attempt to fulfill your needs and/or medicate your pain now?

- What are some other possible strategies to get these needs met that you are willing to experiment with trying?

- What is your motivation in acting out your current behaviors? What caused them in the first place?

- Who can help keep you accountable to these changes you want to make?

- What circumstances and relationships in your life now are holding you back from your goal? Who is helping you achieve it?

- Are you finding yourself falling into patterns of feeling shame and judging yourself? How so?

- What are some ways you can challenge those thoughts, feelings, and reactions?

- Where and with whom are you succeeding?

- Where and with whom are you struggling?

- Who is one person you can apologize to without causing further damage to them? What are you apologizing for?

- What are some ways that you can make amends for how you've hurt this person and betrayed their trust?

- How can you demonstrate long-term change as you progress?

- How will you know when you've succeeded and have been accountable?

- What are some ways that you can give back to help other people who have struggled in the same areas and ways as yourself?

SMART Goal Setting

Okay, sweet. That was a lot. But it gives you a ton of information to make some actionable goals now. I've been using SMART goal setting for [insert a number of decades because I'm really old and shit]. I found when taking the time to use this method with clients, we were way better at knocking shit out of the park. It seems like a lot, but you're already going through a lot, right? You're already a badass survivor who just needs some support to move from surviving to thriving. Stoodis.

Specific

A SMART recovery plan identifies a specific action or event that will take place.

Measurable (in progress and completion)

The description of a SMART recovery plan will allow you to determine your progress towards completion and let you know when you are finished.

Achievable

A SMART recovery plan should be achievable given available resources.

Realistic (in time and skill)

A SMART recovery plan should require you to stretch some beyond your normal routine and regular abilities but allow for likely success based on your skills and the time available.

Time-Based

A SMART recovery plan should state the specific time period in which it will be accomplished.

Questions for consideration:

- What would life look like if your current problems have been resolved?

- How will you know you are on the right path?

- How will you know when you have gotten there?

- What SMART goal do you want to set to help you get started?

Intention Setting

Most of us are used to the idea of goal setting. Goals are about specific, measurable, and quantifiable outcomes. And goal setting is important, but in day-to-day life many things that are out of our control that can affect our goal attainment (Covid-19 in 2020, anyone?).

Intention setting is about how we focus our energy on a day-to-day basis. It's about what we set our minds to notice. If you are looking to purchase a new bike, you are going to notice the bikes around you in a completely different way, right? Intentions are about how we want to interact in the world, what we want to notice, and who we want to be. This will end up supporting our goal attainment. You can consciously pay attention to opportunities to advance your goals, but successful humaning stands apart (and above) our goal achievement. So let's start with our locus of control. What is completely in your control? What is partially in your control? What do you have no control over?

In some way, shape, or form, your answers centered on the fact that you do not have control over the behaviors of others, but you do have control over yourself, right? This is important for intention setting, because whatever you set needs to be grounded in your own locus of control. While "I don't want to argue with anyone" is a nice goal to have, you don't have control over the argumentative nature of someone else. An intention of "I will presume the best intent of those around me" will go a long way to prevent you from starting an argument *and* will go a long way in helping you manage an argument that you get invited to participate in by someone else, right?

Consider setting an intention for the week, whether or not you are doing any goal setting as well. Then notice the following:

- In what ways did you succeed with this intention?

- In what ways did you struggle with it?

- Is this an intention that is of benefit to you?

- Do you want to carry it forward or make any adjustments?

Building Healthy Habits

We don't really think enough about habits. We think we do, but what we are really focusing on are our goals, which are the outcomes we are hoping to achieve. Healthy habits, in comparison, are our *everyday actions that are in service of our goals* (not to mention helping life generally be as manageable as possible). Healthy habits are our building blocks to a healthier life and are often in service of multiple goals.

If you have ever felt like a "new habit" failure, you are not alone. Many of our messages about habit building are simplistic and misrepresented, leading to frustration. One of the biggest ones is the "twenty-one days to change a habit" movement that was hugely popular in the aughts. Research demonstrates that it takes a good three to six months for a new habit to "stick" (meaning, having it become our new normal).

We're having to build a new neural pathway, which requires some heavy trench work for a while. Even then, the old pathways don't go away. They get weeded over a bit, and we become more and more cognizant that we are heading in the wrong direction. But we always have to keep in mind that the old path is still there in our brains and can be reactivated.

That may be more-than-slightly frustrating news, but it's also good news because that means it's true for ALL our neural pathways. If you have been working on your new healthy habit trenches and you fall off for a while? The work you did hasn't disappeared. It's waiting for you to get back on the right path and keep digging. The progress isn't lost entirely. If it's physical exercise, you will be sore again for awhile while your body gets back on track, but your brain didn't lose that progress and remembers what to do.

So let's start with small habits:

What are three incremental changes you can make that are in support of your long-term goals and a healthier life? Be as specific as possible, while trying to allow some flexibility. For example, going walking once a week for twenty minutes is awesome. And Tuesdays may seem like the best day right now, but allow yourself the space to make it Thursday if Tuesday gets totally biffed.

How, *how* can you make each new habit frictionless? Frictionless is the term used to describe making new habits as easy as possible to engage in, in order to give them a fighting chance over the old, established neural pathways. This usually means making environmental changes so you aren't as exhausted by the mental energy these new habits require. For example, I keep healthier but still delicious snacks at my office and in my car. If they are right there, and they are things I like (like cocoa dusted almonds), I will grab those rather than stopping at a gas station and getting something that spikes my blood sugar too much and leaves me nauseous within an hour.

Now, how can you tie each habit to something else you already do that you plan on continuing to do? For example, if your favorite podcast drops every Monday, can you listen to it while you work on organizing your home office? Or even if you can't do things at the same time, you can still plan on doing one right before or after the other. For example, "After I get home, I will turn off the car and meditate for five minutes before I go into the house."

Some other habit-keeping tips:

1) Get an accountability buddy. Tell someone what you are working on and invite them to check in on you and your progress. You'll want to be able to give them a positive report when they do!

2) Don't beat yourself up for not doing it exactly right. If you planned on walking for thirty minutes and were only able to handle twenty? That's still twenty more minutes than before, right?

3) Celebrate your successes, as long as they aren't contradictory to your new habits. If you are working to eat mindfully and recognize your own full signals, rewarding yourself with a binge is a contradictory

habit, right? But there are many other things you can do to treat yourself . . . and they can even still include something really delicious to eat . . . as long as you are able to hold onto your new habit in the process.

4) Keep a habit tracking log. You get to see your progress on paper and sometimes being able to give us our own gold stars feels so positive that it becomes a reward in and of itself. There are tons of habit trackers that you can download as an app, or you can create a spreadsheet, but any notebook and pen will work!

Autogenic Training

One of the most-studied means of self-soothing is called autogenic training. I know, I'm sorry with the ridiculous naming of things because it just means a self-induced relaxation technique that helps soothe the autonomic nervous system, and it's been around for almost a hundred years and has a bunch of research showing its effectiveness in managing anxiety and distress. Autogenic training involves mental repetition (self-coaching) in six systemic exercises around warmth, heaviness, calm and regular heart beat, calm and regular breathing, soft warmth of the upper abdomen, and soothing coolness of the forehead.

To do autogenic training, you start in a comfortable position (sitting upright or laying down) and you close your eyes and either listen to the autogenic prompts (YouTube is good for this) or repeat the ones below to yourself. Most people start with one focus area at a time and build their skills from there (and you'll see how the prompts will help you do this). The six focus areas are:

1. Heaviness in your muscles

2. Warmth in your arms, legs, and other body areas

3. Slower and more relaxed heartbeat

4. Slower and more relaxed breathing

5. Relaxation of the belly

6. Coolness of the forehead

The prompts are designed to connect with each of the six focus areas. The idea is that you say each one to yourself four times before moving on to the next one. The goal is to say them with enough slowness and consideration that it takes about five seconds to repeat the phrase. Then take a three second pause after each statement.

These AI statements are provided by Veterans Affairs (because they use AI training quite often!):

Set 1: Heavy

My right arm is heavy.

My left arm is heavy.

Both of my arms are heavy.

My right leg is heavy.

My left leg is heavy.

Both of my legs are heavy.

My arms and my legs are heavy.

Set 2: Warmth

My right arm is warm.

My left arm is warm.

Both of my arms are warm.

My right leg is warm.

My left leg is warm.

Both of my legs are warm.

My arms and my legs are warm.

Set 3: Calm Heart

My arms are heavy and warm.

My legs are heavy and warm.

My arms and legs are heavy and warm.

I feel calm.

My heart feels warm and pleasant.

My heartbeat is calm and regular.

Set 4: Breathing

My arms are heavy and warm.

My legs are heavy and warm.

My arms and legs are heavy and warm.

I feel calm.

My heartbeat is calm and regular.

My breathing breathes me.

Set 5: Stomach

My arms are heavy and warm.

My legs are heavy and warm.

My arms and legs are heavy and warm.

I feel calm.

My heart feels calm and regular.

My breathing breathes me.

My stomach is soft and warm.

Set 6: Cool Forehead

My arms are heavy and warm.

My legs are heavy and warm.

My arms and legs are heavy and warm.

I feel calm

My heartbeat is calm and regular.

My breathing breathes me.

My stomach is soft and warm. My forehead is cool.

RELAPSE

What Leads to Relapse/Reactivation of Problem Behaviors

*A*nyone trying to change their behavior patterns, whether avoiding relapse or avoiding reactivation of problematic behaviors, knows that certain things activate the desire to use/engage in these behaviors.

Generally, the word "triggers" is used to describe what makes you want to throw fuck-all to the wind and soothe yourself with whatever helped most in the past. The habit loop described below uses the term "cues." Since the word "triggers" is also used to describe situations in which the brain relives a past traumatic event, I use the term "activators" to describe the situations in which all of our progress in recovery gets threatened, and the desire for all our previous behaviors comes rushing back.

Why do we do things we *know* even in the moment are bad for us? Journalist Charles Duhigg in his book *The Power of*

Habit: Why We Do What We Do in Life and Business refers to it as a habit loop, based on research conducted at MIT. A habit loop has three components:

The Cue

The Routine

The Reward

Let's talk about what each of these mean.

The Cue

Every behavior we are trying to change has a cue. As I mentioned above, I use the term *activators* with my clients, by which I mean any event that contributes to the behavioral response we are trying to change. There are multiple things that could be activators, and (yes) there is a lot of overlap between the categories:

Activities: For example, many people associate drinking with going to clubs or parties. The activity and the behavior are so intertwined, engaging in these activities without the other behavior actually upsets the brain.

Situations: This could be things that are stressful that we want to medicate (like fighting with a partner, having to go visit family, getting in trouble at work) or things that we are excited about that we want to celebrate (getting a great grade on an exam that was difficult and stressful, advocating for and getting a raise, etc.)

People: People could be anyone. Anyone who exhausts you so much you want to medicate (Mom called and so now I really need to unwind) or someone who also engages in the same behaviors (the friend who shows up with an eight ball even though you told them you are trying to get your life together).

Places: This is less about the situation and more about the physical place. Like being in your family home, whether your shitty older sibling is there or not (because you REMEMBER them shoving you into the wall you are sitting against right now, how could you not?) or driving past your old school. Any place that brings up strong feelings, good or bad.

Things: This could be anything you associate with use. A can of Fanta orange soda if that is what you used to smoke meth. A shoe sale email if you shop to numb out discomfort.

Thoughts: Because, man, brains are good at talking us into things. And out of other things. And they often mix up which is which. Your thoughts may tell you that you can manage just fine, that eating an entire cheesecake is just a *Golden Girls* vibe, not a means of avoiding difficult feelings. Or maybe it isn't about the use issue, and just about being a trash human who isn't deserving of good things so might as well do stupid things. Any thought that activates you to engage in the behavior you're trying to change.

Emotional States: Just like an activator can be any thought, it can also be any emotion. Happy ones that cue you to celebrate, shitty ones that cue you to medicate. It may be feeling angry or lonely or it may be feeling competent and successful. Emotions are intended to activate us toward action, though in this case it isn't the action that we are going for.

The Routine

The routine is the actual behavior. The thing you are doing, whether an addiction or a behavior that is causing you more harm than good. It becomes so habituated that you don't even recognize what you are doing. Bored and lonely leads to "Let's scroll social media and see what's up," and then you're another hour into double tapping pictures of people you don't know for a little bit of a dopamine boost. Tired and overwhelmed may lead to "Drink your third quad shot iced Americano of the day." The routine is the actual behavior and how you engage in it.

The Reward

The Reward is the actual point. The thing you get out of doing the other thing. It is feeling good. Or relieved. Or safe. A drug that medicates your distress. A behavior that distracts you from reality. Anything that keeps the cycle going.

Okay, then what?

Now this is where things get interesting. If the cue is the first thing, then it seems like the cue is what we should focus on. However, brains are assholes and like to hide that information from us, so we often have to reverse-engineer the situation because it has become so automated we have no idea what's actually going on.

Duhigg's method (framework) actually starts by identifying the routine. Because the routine is the most obvious part, right? It's the actual thing you do, not what incites you to do it or how it feels afterwards. Once you've identified the routine, then you start trying out different rewards. Change up your regular routines and see what helps. You may notice that you do better if you are getting adequate sleep in general. Or notice that you are less likely to engage in the behavior you want to change if you reach out to a friend and get some support and company when feeling anxious. As you are experimenting with rewards, you will start to notice what may be your specific cues. Because now you're paying attention to your own processes right? Once you start isolating some of the big ones you can come up with a more specific plan to manage them when they arise.

SUPPORT

Social Supports

Social support refers to any of the people, groups, and communities that you can access to provide either tangible or intangible assistance to buffer your resilience in times of stress, with resilience just being the term we use for our ability to adapt to adversity without having our whole life go sideways because of it.

There are three types of social support:

Information Support: Informational support is when someone has the knowledge or the hook-up on the resources you need to resolve a particular problem. I recently had a friend who needs therapy but doesn't have health insurance or a ton of money because he's in school. I gave him the info on where to go, who to ask for when he got there, and what to say to access a particular therapy grant. He just needed some resources, then he did all the work.

Material Support: Material support is tangible help. Like covering part of someone's rent for them because they didn't get enough hours at their job, or helping them fix something they couldn't afford to have fixed, or giving them a ride to a job interview because the site is off the bus line. This is the kind of support that can be measured in some way.

Emotional Support: This is the type of support that provides you space for your stress, anxiety, anger, depression or general overwhelm. These are the people to whom you have a sense of connectedness, of being seen and understood. They are empathetic and supportive without letting you off the hook if you are heading toward a bad decision (or already made one) but provide compassion and encouragement while you work to stay or get back on track.

- How could social support be of benefit to you with your current struggles?

- What people or groups/communities can you access for social support?

- Which type of these supports are offered by these individuals or groups? How do each of these supports help you? Or how could they if you reached out?

- What gets in the way of your accessing these supports?

- In what specific ways could you work around these access issues? How else could you better utilize these supports?

What If I Really Don't Have Any? Or Have Very Little Social Support?

Many people have little to no social support in their lives. I hear this regularly, and it breaks my heart. So let's talk about ways of building social support.

Make an effort to reconnect with family and friends that you have lost touch with over time (unless, of course, they've asked you not to). This doesn't mean five minutes into a conversation hitting them up for a ride to the airport—just relationship building for its own sake. Start prioritizing the good people in your life, and being social supports for them. Don't even know where to start? It's okay to keep it vague and start sending out texts or emails with something like:

Hey! I know I haven't been around much. I've been pretty isolated and struggling, and I'm working on reaching out to the people I care about to say I'm sorry for that and I want to do better. No response necessary if you aren't inclined, but I'd love to hear what you've been up to lately!

This is a really helpful "getting back out there" tool for any reason . . . depression, anxiety, grief . . . anything that has kept you under the covers instead of out in the world.

Join a support group. Find people who are working through issues the same or similar to yours and find space in their meetings. Ugh, I know. But seriously, people who "get it" can be so helpful. You don't have to do anything formal or get a sponsor at a twelve-step meeting. Just finding people who are out there working to improve their lives and embracing the vulnerability it takes to get some support in doing so? Hella awesome.

Get more active in your community in general. Do things you are interested in trying or used to do and really miss. This could be joining a gaming group, a running club, or a cooking class. Maybe it's volunteering at the animal shelter or for a local political cause. Whatever. Even if you don't make any new friends right away, activities like these won't feel like wasted time because you had fun and pushed yourself out of your comfort zone. Which is a healthy coping skill in and of itself.

Professional supports are also supports. Doctors, therapists, case managers, etc. It's our literal job to help you problem-solve these issues that are chipping away at your resilience. Let us know!

- Who are two or three people that you can reach out to with a message offering to reconnect?

- What kind of support group might make sense and where can you search for options or who can you ask about options?

- What is some level of community involvement that you've always been interested in trying when you had time (since this is the perfect opportunity to make some time)?

- What professional care do you have available?

- What might be some other professional care options that may help?

- Where can you go to find out more about accessing them?

Supporting Others' Recovery

You may be reading this book because someone in your life who you absolutely adore is struggling with an addiction or out of control behavior. You are trying to figure out how to support them without hitting them over the head with this book. Which I appreciate . . . even paperbacks can be painful when thrown from a distance.

First of all, thank you for caring. Caring more about them than they have the capacity to care for themselves is a terrifying space to be in. It's a rough situation to be in, and I appreciate you trying to find ways to be helpful and supportive. The one thing I can tell you, from a bazillion years of first-hand experience is that you can't work harder than they are working for themselves. You can provide all kinds of ideas and strategies and support. But you can't enforce someone's recovery, at least for very long. They have to be willing to do the work. So everything I am going to suggest in this section was designed with the acronym FRAP in mind. We've got to love and support people without FRAPing them. To not FRAP means you don't fix, rescue, advise, or project:

Fix: People aren't broken.

Rescue: This is feeding people fish, not teaching them how to fish.

Advise: This is only okay if people ask for it, but often they are asking to be rescued.

Project: It's better to get curious about what's going on inside you.

Okay, now let's talk about what some strategies might look like in our real (and FRAP-free) lives.

What If You Want to Talk to Them about Their Use?

Don't have the conversation when they are altered. Meaning they aren't drunk or high. This may be hard to judge, especially if they are good at using without seeming altered. You may have to pay attention to their patterns a bit to get a good idea. It's also really helpful to have as quiet and neutral a setting as possible. Talk to them about your concerns from the point of view of how their life is being impacted, especially around the things that matter to them. It may be their relationship with you or with their kids, or that they are now struggling at a job they used to love. Demonstrate how use may be replacing what is most valuable to them in this regard. They may not care about themselves, but they may care about others.

It is also really helpful to have some resources ready to go if they agree to give treatment a try. But don't make appointments without telling them and then drag them to see a therapist that they didn't know they were scheduled to see.

As one such therapist can tell you, this doesn't go well. I've learned to ask that question explicitly and upset some people by refusing to schedule a client for a surprise session. Yes, even if you are more than happy to pay for the appointment. It's a "working harder than they are" issue again. You can't trick them into the work, they have to be willing to give it a whirl. Talk about the resources you found and offer to facilitate them getting there, but ultimately it is their decision to go or not go.

Whether you get somewhere or not, be prepared for a lot of emotional fallout. Think about all the possible ways they may react, and plan on how you will respond so you can be proactive instead of reactive in the face of anger, tears, etc. It may also feel shitty and exhausting for *you* as well. You're trying to help and you may get berated for your involvement. Or met with stony silence. Or any number of un-great responses. You need to be ready to take care of yourself emotionally, not just them.

What If Talking to Them Isn't a Viable Option Right Now? Or Didn't Work?

I'm so sorry. Being in a space of "not doing" is the hardest thing, isn't it? And if this is someone close to you, you may be feeling the effects of their use on your life. They may live in your house, and you may have safety concerns. Or they don't stay with you but are so impacted by their use that they aren't great to be around. They don't follow through on commitments, they're unkind to you, they are asking for resources (like money, the use of your car, etc.) that you know is going to support their behavior. Now what?

First of all, consider getting your own support. In the information and treatment resources section of this book are the websites for Al-Anon and Nar-Anon. These are peer-led groups of family members and other loved ones of people who have problems with alcohol (Al-Anon) or drugs (Nar-Anon). Depending on your level of involvement, this support may be of benefit to maintaining loving boundaries.

If those groups aren't helpful (or are not related to the issue at hand), seeing a therapist or talking to a trusted wise friend about setting boundaries around your relationship could be of huge benefit. It may include having to look at your level of legal liability for their use (if the person in question is a minor child you are the guardian of, or if you are renting and they live with you and there is a no use or paraphernalia policy where you live). It could also be helpful to think pragmatically about harm reduction around their use, such as keeping naloxone with you if they use opioids or other drugs that have been connected to fentanyl contamination. I know this is *a lot* to think about it if you are new to this topic, which is why talking to someone who isn't new but is empathetic could help you feel much better about your experiences and your options.

Seriously, though, no matter what hard decisions you may have to end up making? I'm so glad you care. So many people don't. Thanks for being one of the good guys.

INFORMATION AND TREATMENT RESOURCES

*W*ithin the section on harm reduction planning are more websites to help you get clean needles, fentanyl test strips, PrEP medication and the like. Don't forget to check out that section as well, if you haven't already.

SAMHSA's National Helpline

A confidential, free, 24-hour-a-day, 365-day-a-year, information service, in English and Spanish

1-800-662-HELP (4357)

TTY: 1-800-487-4889

SAMHSA Treatment Locator

The treatment locator website is designed to help you find programs in your area. If you want more specific information about program funding, you may want to call your local 211 line instead (info below).

samhsa.gov/find-treatment

211 Community Resource Line

This is a really good starting point for finding addictions treatment programs that are fully funded if you don't have adequate insurance coverage and can't afford the expense of out-of-pocket care.

211.org

Alcoholics Anonymous

Alcoholics Anonymous is a fellowship of people who come together to solve their drinking problem. It doesn't cost anything to attend AA meetings. There are no age or education requirements to participate. Membership is open to anyone who wants to do something about their drinking problem. AA's primary purpose is to help alcoholics to achieve sobriety. Check out their website for information on meetings.

aa.org

Alcoholics Anonymous Resource Center

AlcoholicsAnonymous.com is not affiliated with Alcoholics Anonymous World Services, Inc. but operates as a resource center. The purpose of this site is to provide information and social networking to support our fellow AA members. Check out their website for finding meetings in your area.

SMART Recovery

SMART stands for Self-Management and Recovery Training, A twelve-step alternative based in cognitive behavioral therapy that is used for substances and gambling addiction. Check out their website for meeting information.

smartrecovery.org

LifeRing Secular Recovery

LifeRing Secular Recovery is an organization of people who share practical experiences and sobriety support. There are as many ways to live free of illicit or non-medically indicated drugs and alcohol as there are stories of successful sober people. Many LifeRing members attend other kinds of meetings or recovery programs, and we honor those decisions. Some have had negative experiences in attempting to find help elsewhere, but most people soon find that LifeRing's emphasis on the positive, practical, and present-day can turn anger and despair into hope and resolve. LifeRing respectfully embraces what works for each individual. Check out their website for information on meetings, their podcast, and email groups.

lifering.org

SOS (Secular Organizations for Sobriety)

Secular Organizations for Sobriety (SOS) is a nonprofit network of autonomous, non-professional, local groups dedicated solely to helping individuals achieve and maintain sobriety/abstinence from alcohol and drug addiction. Check out their website for information about in person and online meetings.

sossobriety.org

Moderation Management (MM)

Moderation Management™ is a lay-led nonprofit dedicated to reducing the harm caused by the misuse of alcohol. Check out their website for information on meetings and their online community.

moderation.org

Women for Sobriety (WFS)/New Life Program

Women For Sobriety (WFS) is both an organization and a self-help program (also called the New Life Program) for women with Substance Use Disorders. Founded in 1975, it was the first national self-help program for addiction recovery developed to address the unique needs of women., finding that the physiological needs of addiction recovery are similar across gender lines, but the emotional needs can be different. WFS welcomes all women, not just cis women into services. Based upon the thirteen Acceptance Statements, it can stand alone or be used along with other recovery supports simultaneously. Check out their website for information about meetings, conferences, and their online forum.

womenforsobriety.org

White Bison Wellbriety Movement

A sustainable grassroots Wellbriety Movement that provides culturally based healing for the next seven generations of Indigenous people through culturally based principles, values, and teachings that support healthy community development and servant leadership and to support healing from alcohol, substance abuse, co-occurring disorders, and intergenerational trauma. You do not need to be Indigenous to attend, but be prepared for stepwork that is based on the concept of the medicine wheel. Check out their website for information on meetings and conferences.

whitebison.org

Refuge Recovery

Refuge Recovery is a practice, a process, a set of tools, a treatment, and a path to healing addiction and the suffering caused by addiction based on the four noble truths of Buddhism. Check out their website for information on in person and online meetings, retreats, and conferences.

refugerecovery.org

Recovery Dharma

Recovery Dharma is a peer-led movement and community unified by trust in the potential of each of us to recover and find freedom from the suffering of addiction. They believe that the traditional Buddhist teachings, often referred to as the Dharma, offer a powerful approach to healing from addiction and living a life of true freedom. Check out their website for information on meetings, retreats, and conferences.

recoverydharma.org

Al-Anon Family Groups

These meetings are designed for individuals who have a loved one with an alcohol use disorder, based more on the traditional twelve-step model. Check out their website for information on meetings, retreats, and conferences.

al-anon.org

Nar-Anon

Nar-Anon is like Al-Anon but more specific to family members whose loved one is struggling with drugs, not alcohol.

nar-anon.org

Gamblers Anonymous

GA is a fellowship of people who share their experience, strength, and hope with each other that they may solve their common problem and help others to recover from a gambling problem. The only requirement for membership is a desire to stop gambling. Check out their website for information on in person, phone, and online meetings.

gamblersanonymous.org

Gam-Anon International Service

Gam-Anon is a twelve-step self-help fellowship of people who have been affected by the gambling problem of another. Check out their website for meeting information.

gam-anon.org

REFERENCES

Adrian, M., Berk, M. S., Korslund, K., Whitlock, K., McCauley, E., & Linehan, M. (2018). "Parental validation and invalidation predict adolescent self-harm." *Professional Psychology: Research and Practice, 49*(4), 274–281. doi.org/10.1037/pro0000200

Alavi, S. S., Ferdosi, M., Jannatifard, F., Eslami, M., Alaghemandan, H., & Setare, M. (2012). "Behavioral Addiction versus Substance Addiction: Correspondence of Psychiatric and Psychological Views." *International Journal of Preventive Medicine, 3*(4), 290–294.

"Alcohol and thiamine." Alcohol-related thiamine deficiency— Alcohol and Drug Foundation. (n.d.). Retrieved April 7, 2023, from adf.org.au/insights/alcohol-related-thiamine-deficiency/

American Psychiatric Association (2022). *Diagnostic and Statistical Manual of Mental Disorders, Fifth Edition Text Revision: DSM-5-TR.*

Anton R. F. (2008). "Naltrexone for the management of alcohol dependence." *The New England Journal of Medicine, 359*(7), 715–721. doi.org/10.1056/NEJMct0801733

Autogenic Training. Veterans Affairs. (n.d.). Retrieved February 27, 2023, from va.gov/WHOLEHEALTH/Veteran-Handouts/docs/AutogenicTraining-508Final-9-5-2018.pdf

Berczik, K., Szabó, A., Griffiths, M. D., Kurimay, T., Kun, B., Urbán, R., & Demetrovics, Z. (2012). "Exercise Addiction: Symptoms, Diagnosis, Epidemiology, and Etiology. *Substance Use & Misuse, 47*(4), 403–417. doi.org/10.3109/10826084.2011.639120

Bem, D. J. (1972). "Self-Perception Theory." *Advances in Experimental Social Psychology*, Volume 6, 1–62. doi. org/10.1016/s0065-2601(08)60024-6

Berry, M. S., Sweeney, M. M., Dolan, S. B., Johnson, P. S., Pennybaker, S. J., Rosch, K. S., & Johnson, M. W. (2021). "Attention-Deficit/Hyperactivity Disorder Symptoms Are Associated with Greater Delay Discounting of Condom-Protected Sex and Money." *Archives of Sexual Behavior,* 50(1), 191–204. doi.org/10.1007/s10508-020-01698-8

Cash, H., Rae, C. D., Steel, A. H., & Winkler, A. (2012). "Internet Addiction: A Brief Summary of Research and Practice." *Current Psychiatry Reviews*, 8(4), 292–298. doi. org/10.2174/157340012803520513

Brady, K. T., Haynes, L. F., Hartwell, K. J., & Killeen, T. K. (2013). "Substance Use Disorders and Anxiety: A Treatment Challenge for Social Workers." *Social Work in Public Health*, 28(3-4), 407–423. doi.org/10.1080/19371918.2013.774675

Brewer, J. A., & Potenza, M. N. (2008). "The Neurobiology and Genetics of Impulse Control Disorders: Relationships to Drug Addictions." *Biochemical Pharmacology*, 75(1), 63–75. doi.org/10.1016/j.bcp.2007.06.043

Brown, D. (n.d.). "How Understanding Neurodiversity in Borderline Can Help." HealthyPlace. Retrieved January 8, 2023, from healthyplace.com/blogs/borderline/2022/4/how-understanding-neurodiversity-in-borderline-can-help#:~:text=Did%20you%20know%20that%20neurodiversity,health%20community%20and%20evolving%20quickly.

Buprenorphine (trade names: Buprenex®, Suboxone®, Subutex® , Zubsolv . . . (n.d.). Retrieved January 17, 2023, from deadiversion.usdoj.gov/drug_chem_info/buprenorphine.pdf

Buprenorphine. SAMHSA. (n.d.). Retrieved January 18, 2023, from samhsa.gov/medication-assisted-treatment/medications-counseling-related-conditions/buprenorphine

Cardona, N., Madigan, & Sauer (2021). "How Minority Stress Becomes Traumatic Invalidation: An Emotion-Focused Conceptualization of Minority Stress in Sexual and Gender

Minority People." *Clinical Psychology Science and Practice*. 29. 10.1037/cps0000054.

Center for Substance Abuse Treatment. "Incorporating Alcohol Pharmacotherapies Into Medical Practice." Rockville (MD): Substance Abuse and Mental Health Services Administration (US); 2009. (Treatment Improvement Protocol (TIP) Series, No. 49.) Chapter 4—Oral Naltrexone. Available from: ncbi. nlm.nih.gov/books/NBK64042/

Chen, M. H., Hsu, J. W., Huang, K. L., Bai, Y. M., Ko, N. Y., Su, T. P., Li, C. T., Lin, W. C., Tsai, S. J., Pan, T. L., Chang, W. H., & Chen, T. J. (2018). "Sexually Transmitted Infection Among Adolescents and Young Adults With Attention-Deficit/Hyperactivity Disorder: A Nationwide Longitudinal Study." *Journal of the American Academy of Child and Adolescent Psychiatry, 57*(1), 48–53. doi.org/10.1016/j.jaac.2017.09.438

Center for Drug Evaluation and Research. (n.d.). Bupropion hydrochloride information. US Food and Drug Administration. Retrieved March 29, 2023, from fda.gov/drugs/postmarket-drug-safety-information-patients-and-providers/bupropion hydrochloride-marketed-wellbutrin-zyban-and-generics-information

Centers for Disease Control and Prevention. (2022, December 28). Lifesaving naloxone. Centers for Disease Control and Prevention. Retrieved January 18, 2023, from cdc.gov/stopoverdose/naloxone/index.html

Counseling Center. The University of Toledo. (n.d.). Retrieved October 26, 2022, from utoledo.edu/studentaffairs/counseling/selfhelp/substanceuse/marijuanatolerancewithdrawal.html

Courtwright D. T. (2004). "The Controlled Substances Act: How a 'Big Tent' Reform Became a Punitive Drug Law. *Drug and Alcohol Dependence, 76*(1), 9–15. doi.org/10.1016/j.drugalcdep.2004.04.012

Daniels, C., Aluso, A., Burke-Shyne, N., Koram, K., Rajagopalan, S., Robinson, I., Shelly, S., Shirley-Beavan, S., & Tandon, T. (2021). "Decolonizing Drug Policy." *Harm Reduction Journal, 18*(1), 120. doi.org/10.1186/s12954-021-00564-7

Escohotado, A. (1999). *A Brief History of Drugs: From the Stone Age to the Stoned Age*. Park Street Press.

Frayn, M., Livshits, S., & Knäuper, B. (2018). "Emotional Eating and Weight Regulation: A Qualitative Study of Compensatory Behaviors and Concerns." *Journal of Eating Disorders*, 6, 23. doi.org/10.1186/s40337-018-0210-6

Ferrajão PC. (2020). The role of parental emotional validation and invalidation on children's clinical symptoms: A study with children exposed to intimate partner violence. tandfonline.com/doi/abs/10.1080/15379418.2020.1731399

Freimuth, M., Moniz, S., & Kim, S. R. (2011). "Clarifying Exercise Addiction: Differential Diagnosis, Co-Occurring Disorders, and Phases of Addiction." *International Journal of Environmental Research and Public Health*, 8(10), 4069–4081. doi.org/10.3390/ijerph8104069

The Freedom Center. (2022, February 11). "What are the differences between PHP & IOP Treatment?" The Freedom Center. Retrieved January 11, 2023, from thefreedomcenter. com/what-are-the-differences-between-php-and-iop-treatment/

Gilbert, D. T., Lieberman, M. D., Morewedge, C. K., & Wilson, T. D. (2004). "The Peculiar Longevity of Things Not So Bad. *Psychological Science*, 15(1), 14–19. doi.org/10.1111/j.0963-7214.2004.01501003.x

Griffin J. B., . "Loss of Control." In: Walker HK, Hall WD, Hurst JW, editors. *Clinical Methods: The History, Physical, and Laboratory Examinations*. 3rd edition. Boston: Butterworths; 1990. Chapter 204. Available from: ncbi.nlm.nih.gov/books/NBK317/

Harm reduction. SAMHSA. (n.d.). Retrieved February 27, 2023, from samhsa.gov/find-help/harm-reduction

Hartney, E. (2022, August 25). DSM 5 Criteria for Substance Use Disorders. Verywell Mind. Retrieved January 4, 2023, from verywellmind.com/dsm-5-criteria-for-substance-use-disorders-21926

Hasin, D. S., O'Brien, C. P., Auriacombe, M., Borges, G., Bucholz, K., Budney, A., Compton, W. M., Crowley, T., Ling, W., Petry, N. M., Schuckit, M., & Grant, B. F. (2013). "DSM-5 Criteria for Substance Use Disorders: Recommendations and Rationale." *The American Journal of Psychiatry*, 170(8), 834–851. doi.org/10.1176/appi.ajp.2013.12060782

Hasin, D., Paykin, A., Meydan, J., & Grant, B. (2000). "Withdrawal and Tolerance: Prognostic Significance in DSM-IV Alcohol Dependence." *Journal of Studies on Alcohol*, 61(3), 431–438. doi.org/10.15288/jsa.2000.61.431

Hosain, G. M., Berenson, A. B., Tennen, H., Bauer, L. O., & Wu, Z. H. (2012). "Attention Deficit Hyperactivity Symptoms and Risky Sexual Behavior in Young Adult Women." *Journal of Women's Health* (2002), 21(4), 463–468. doi.org/10.1089/jwh.2011.2825

Hu, W., Morris, B., Carrasco, A., & Kroener, S. (2015). "Effects of Acamprosate on Attentional Set-Shifting and Cellular Function in the Prefrontal Cortex of Chronic Alcohol-Exposed Mice." *Alcoholism, Clinical and Experimental Research*, 39(6), 953–961. doi.org/10.1111/acer.12722

Institute of Medicine (US) Committee on Federal Regulation of Methadone Treatment; Rettig RA, Yarmolinsky A, editors. Federal Regulation of Methadone Treatment. Washington (DC): National Academies Press (US); 1995. Executive Summary. Available from: ncbi.nlm.nih.gov/books/NBK232111/

Institute of Medicine (US) Committee on Opportunities in Drug Abuse Research. Pathways of Addiction: Opportunities in Drug Abuse Research. Washington (DC): National Academies Press (US); 1996. 5, Etiology. Available from: ncbi.nlm.nih.gov/books/NBK232972/

Johnson, A. (2000). *Eating By the Light of the Moon*. Carlsbad, CA: Gurze Books.

Konttinen, H., Van Strien, T., Männistö, S., Jousilahti, P., & Haukkala, A. (2019). "Depression, Emotional Eating and Long-Term Weight Changes: A Population-Based Prospective Study." *International Journal of Behavioral Nutrition and Physical Activity*, 16(1). doi:10.1186/s12966-019-0791-8

Kumar, M., & Mondal, A. (2018). A Study on Internet Addiction and Its Relation to Psychopathology and Self-Esteem Among College Students. *Industrial Psychiatry Journal*, 27(1), 61–66. doi.org/10.4103/ipj.ipj_61_17

Kuppili, P. P., Parmar, A., Gupta, A., & Balhara, Y. P. S. (2018). "Role of Yoga in Management of Substance-use Disorders: A

Narrative Review." *Journal of Neurosciences in Rural Practice*, 9(1), 117–122. doi.org/10.4103/jnrp.jnrp_243_17

Kuss, D. J., & Griffiths, M. D. (2011). "Internet Gaming Addiction: A Systematic Review of Empirical Research." *International Journal of Mental Health and Addiction*, 10(2), 278–296. doi.org/10.1007/s11469-011-9318-5

Johnson KC, et al. (2019). Invalidation experiences among non-binary adolescents. tandfonline.com/doi/abs/10.1080/00224499.2019.1608422

Lee, S. S. M., Keng, S.-L., Yeo, G. C., & Hong, R. Y. (2022). "Parental Invalidation and Its Associations with Borderline Personality Disorder Symptoms: A Multivariate Meta-Analysis." *Personality Disorders: Theory, Research, and Treatment*, 13(6), 572–582. doi.org/10.1037/per0000523

Leotti, L. A., Iyengar, S. S., & Ochsner, K. N. (2010). "Born to Choose: The Origins and Value of the Need for Control." *Trends in Cognitive Sciences*, 14(10), 457–463. doi.org/10.1016/j.tics.2010.08.001

Leslie, KM, Canadian Paediatric Society, Adolescent Health Committee. "Harm Reduction: An Approach to Reducing Risky Health Behaviours in Adolescents. (2008). *Paediatrics & Child Health*, 13(1), 53–60. doi.org/10.1093/pch/13.1.53

Levit, M., Weinstein, A., Weinstein, Y., Tzur-Bitan, D., & Weinstein, A. (2018). "A Study on the Relationship Between Exercise Addiction, Abnormal Eating Attitudes, Anxiety and Depression among Athletes in Israel. *Journal of Behavioral Addictions*, 7(3), 800–805. doi.org/10.1556/2006.7.2018.83

Linehan, M. (2017). *DBT Skills Training Manual*. Guilford Press.

Łukawski, K., Rusek, M., & Czuczwar, S. J. (2019). "Can Pharmacotherapy Play a Role in Treating Internet Addiction Disorder?" *Expert Opinion on Pharmacotherapy*, 20(11), 1299–1301. doi.org/10.1080/14656566.2019.1612366

Logan, D. E., & Marlatt, G. A. (2010). "Harm Reduction Therapy: A Practice-Friendly Review of Research." *Journal of Clinical Psychology*, 66(2), 201–214. doi.org/10.1002/jclp.20669

Mason, B. J., & Heyser, C. J. (2010). "Acamprosate: A Prototypic Neuromodulator in the Treatment of Alcohol Dependence."

CNS & Neurological Disorders Drug Targets, 9(1), 23–32. doi. org/10.2174/187152710790966641

Medications, Counseling, and Related Conditions. SAMHSA. (n.d.). Retrieved December 29, 2022, from samhsa.gov/medication-assisted-treatment/medications-counseling-related-conditions

Maté, G. (2021). *In the Realm of Hungry Ghosts: Close Encounters with Addiction.* Vintage Canada.

Maté, G. (2021) *The Wisdom of Trauma.* Film. Retrieved February 27, 2023, from thewisdomoftrauma.com

Mayo Foundation for Medical Education and Research. (2023, February 1). *Varenicline (oral route) proper use.* Mayo Clinic. Retrieved March 29, 2023, from mayoclinic.org/drugs-supplements/varenicline-oral-route/proper-use/drg-20068324#:~:text=You%20should%20set%20a%20date,8%20and%2035%20of%20treatment.

Michaels, T. I., Stone, E., Singal, S., Novakovic, V., Barkin, R. L., & Barkin, S. (2021). "Brain Reward Circuitry: The Overlapping Neurobiology of Trauma and Substance Use Disorders." *World Journal of Psychiatry*, 11(6), 222–231. doi. org/10.5498/wjp.v11.i6.222

Mitchell, K. D., & Higgins, L. J. (2016). "Combating Opioid Overdose with Public Access to Naloxone." *Journal of Addictions Nursing*, 27(3), 160–179. doi.org/10.1097/JAN.0000000000000132

Moeller, F. G., Barratt, E. S., Dougherty, D. M., Schmitz, J. M., & Swann, A. C. (2001). "Psychiatric Aspects of Impulsivity." *The American Journal of Psychiatry*, 158(11), 1783–1793. doi. org/10.1176/appi.ajp.158.11.1783

Morgan, W. P. (1979). "Negative addiction in Runners." *The Physician and Sportsmedicine*, 7(2), 55–77. doi.org/10.1080/00913847.1979.11948436

National Survey on Drug Use and health. SAMHSA.gov. (n.d.). Retrieved December 9, 2022, from samhsa.gov/data/data-we-collect/nsduh-national-survey-drug-use-and-health

Morrison, J. R. (2016). *The First Interview.* Guilford Press.

Morrison, J. R. (2017). *Diagnosis Made Easier: Principles and Techniques for Mental Health Clinicians.* Guilford Press.

Morrison, J. R., (2017). DSM-5 Made Easy: The Clinician's Guide to Diagnosis. Guildford Press.

Musetti, A., Cattivelli, R., Giacobbi, M., Zuglian, P., Ceccarini, M., Capelli, F., Pietrabissa, G., & Castelnuovo, G. (2016). "Challenges in Internet Addiction Disorder: Is a Diagnosis Feasible or Not?" *Frontiers in Psychology*, 7, 842. doi. org/10.3389/fpsyg.2016.00842

Santos, V. A., Freire, R., Zugliani, M., Cirillo, P., Santos, H. H., Nardi, A. E., & King, A. L. (2016). "Treatment of Internet Addiction with Anxiety Disorders: Treatment Protocol and Preliminary Before-After Results Involving Pharmacotherapy and Modified Cognitive Behavioral Therapy." *JMIR Research Protocols*, 5(1), e46. doi.org/10.2196/resprot.5278

Nicola, M. Correia, H. Ditchburn, G. & Drummond, P. (2021) "Invalidation of Chronic Pain: A Thematic Analysis of Pain Narratives. *Disability and Rehabilitation*, 43:6, 861-869, DOI: 10.1080/09638288.2019.1636888

NIDA. 2021, April 13. Is naloxone accessible? . Retrieved from nida.nih.gov/publications/research-reports/medications-to-treat-opioid-addiction/naloxone-accessible on 2023, January 16

Nielsen, A., Dusek, J. A., Taylor-Swanson, L., & Tick, H. (2022). "Acupuncture Therapy as an Evidence-Based Nonpharmacologic Strategy for Comprehensive Acute Pain Care: The Academic Consortium Pain Task Force White Paper Update." *Pain Medicine* (Malden, Mass.), 23(9), 1582–1612. doi.org/10.1093/pm/pnac056

Nguyen-Rodriguez, S. T., Unger, J. B., & Spruijt-Metz, D. (2009). "Psychological Determinants of Emotional Eating in Adolescence." *Eating Disorders*, 17(3), 211–224. doi. org/10.1080/10640260902848543

Nutrition and Addiction Recovery. Recovery.org. (2022, November 15). Retrieved April 7, 2023, from recovery.org/treatment-therapy/nutrition/

Owusu-Bempah, A., & Luscombe, A. (2021). "Race, Cannabis and the Canadian War on Drugs: An Examination of Cannabis Arrest Data by Race in Five Cities. *The International Journal on Drug Policy*, 91, 102937. doi.org/10.1016/j.drugpo.2020.102937

Ramirez-Garcia, M.P., Leclerc-Loiselle, J., Genest, C. *et al.* "Effectiveness of Autogenic Training on Psychological Well-Being and Quality of Life in Adults Living with Chronic Physical Health Problems: A Protocol for a Systematic Review of Rct." *Syst Rev 9*, 74 (2020). doi.org/10.1186/s13643-020-01336-3

Regan, T., & Tubman, J. (2020). "Attention Deficit Hyperactivity Disorder (ADHD) Subtypes, Co-Occurring Psychiatric Symptoms and Sexual Risk Behaviors among Adolescents Receiving Substance Abuse Treatment." *Substance Use & Misuse, 55*(1), 119–132. doi.org/10.1080/10826084.2019.1657895

Removal of data waiver (X-waiver) requirement. SAMHSA. (n.d.). Retrieved January 18, 2023, from samhsa.gov/medication-assisted-treatment/removal-data-waiver-requirement

RxList. (2022, August 11). Types of anti-anxiety drugs (anxiolytics): Uses, side effects, interaction, supplement, pregnancy. RxList. Retrieved January 18, 2023, from rxlist.com/anti-anxiety_drugs_anxiolytics/drugs-condition.htm

Schreiber, L., Odlaug, B. L., & Grant, J. E. (2011). "Impulse Control Disorders: Updated Review of Clinical Characteristics and Pharmacological Management." *Frontiers in Psychiatry, 2*, 1. doi.org/10.3389/fpsyt.2011.00001

Serenko, A., & Turel, O. (2020). "Directing Technology Addiction Research in Information Systems." *ACM SIGMIS Database: The DATABASE for Advances in Information Systems, 51*(3), 81–96. doi.org/10.1145/3410977.3410982

Stokes M, Abdijadid S. "Disulfiram." [Updated 2022 Oct 24]. In: StatPearls [Internet]. Treasure Island (FL): StatPearls Publishing; 2022 Jan. Available from: ncbi.nlm.nih.gov/books/NBK459340/

Substance abuse and mental health services administration. (n.d.). Retrieved January 11, 2023, from store.samhsa.gov/sites/default/files/d7/priv/sma15-4131.pdf

Szabo, A., Griffiths, M. D., de La Vega Marcos, R., Mervó, B., & Demetrovics, Z. (2015). "Methodological and Conceptual Limitations in Exercise Addiction Research." *The Yale Journal of Biology and Medicine, 88*(3), 303–308.

"Topic: Inpatient Care." *AHRQ*. (n.d.). Retrieved January 11, 2023, from ahrq.gov/topics/inpatient-care.html

Trutti, A. C., Mulder, M. J., Hommel, B., & Forstmann, B. U. (2019). "Functional Neuroanatomical Review of the Ventral Tegmental Area." *NeuroImage*, 191, 258–268. doi.org/10.1016/j.neuroimage.2019.01.062

U.S. Department of Health and Human Services. (n.d.). "Alcohol Use Disorder: A Comparison Between DSM–IV and DSM–5." National Institute on Alcohol Abuse and Alcoholism. Retrieved December 9, 2022, from niaaa.nih.gov/publications/brochures-and-fact-sheets/alcohol-use-disorder-comparison-between-dsm

U.S. Department of Health and Human Services. (2022, November 1). *Harm reduction*. National Institutes of Health. Retrieved February 27, 2023, from nida.nih.gov/research-topics/harm-reduction

U.S. Department of Health and Human Services. (2022, September 27). Part 1: The connection between Substance Use Disorders and mental illness. National Institutes of Health. Retrieved January 8, 2023, from nida.nih.gov/publications/research-reports/common-comorbidities-substance-use-disorders/part-1-connection-between-substance-use-disorders-mental-illness

U.S. Department of Health and Human Services. (n.d.). Wernicke-Korsakoff syndrome. National Institute of Neurological Disorders and Stroke. Retrieved April 7, 2023, from ninds.nih.gov/health-information/disorders/wernicke-korsakoff-syndrome#:~:text=Treatment%20involves%20replacement%20of%20thiamine,drug%20therapy%20is%20also%20recommended.

U.S. National Library of Medicine. (n.d.). Substance use recovery and Diet: Medlineplus medical encyclopedia. MedlinePlus. Retrieved April 7, 2023, from medlineplus.gov/ency/article/002149.htm

Wang, A. R., Kuijper, F. M., Barbosa, D. A. N., Hagan, K. E., Lee, E., Tong, E., Choi, E. Y., McNab, J. A., Bohon, C., & Halpern, C. H. (2023). Human habit neural circuitry may be perturbed in eating disorders. Science translational medicine, 15(689), eabo4919. doi.org/10.1126/scitranslmed.abo4919

Wang, Q., Lin, J., Yang, P., Liang, Y., Lu, D., Wang, K., Gan, W., Fu, J., Gan, Z., Ma, M., Wu, P., He, F., Pang, J., & Tang, H. (2020). "Effect of Massage on the TLR4 Signalling Pathway in Rats with Neuropathic Pain." *Pain Research & Management*, 2020, 8309745. doi.org/10.1155/2020/8309745

"What Is Naltrexone?": UAMS Psychiatric Research Institute. (n.d.). Retrieved January 18, 2023, from psychiatry.uams.edu/clinical-care/cast/what-is-naltrexone/"

WebMD. (n.d.). "Dependence Vs. Addiction: What's the Difference? WebMD. Retrieved November 10, 2022, from webmd.com/connect-to-care/addiction-treatment-recovery/dependence-versus-addiction

"What Is Psychological Dependence?" American Addiction Centers. (2021, October 19). Retrieved December 9, 2022, from americanaddictioncenters.org/the-addiction-cycle/psychological-dependence

Winkie, L. (2020, July 13). Here's how loot box & microtransaction addiction destroys lives. IGN. Retrieved January 8, 2023, from ign.com/articles/heres-how-loot-box-addiction-destroys-lives

Witkiewitz, K., Litten, R. Z., & Leggio, L. (2019). Advances in the science and treatment of alcohol use disorder. *Science Advances*, 5(9). doi.org/10.1126/sciadv.aax4043

World Health Organization. (n.d.). Gaming disorder. World Health Organization. Retrieved January 8, 2023, from who.int/standards/classifications/frequently-asked-questions/gaming-disorder#:~:text=Gaming%20disorder%20is%20defined%20in,the%20extent%20that%20gaming%20takes

Zhang, J., Li, Z., Li, Z., Li, J., Hu, Q., Xu, J., & Yu, H. (2021). "Progress of Acupuncture Therapy in Diseases Based on Magnetic Resonance Image Studies: A Literature Review." *Frontiers in Human Neuroscience*, 15, 694919. doi.org/10.3389/fnhum.2021.694919

ABOUT THE AUTHOR

Faith G. Harper, LPC-S, ACS, ACN, is a badass, funny lady with a PhD. She's a licensed professional counselor, board supervisor, certified sexologist, and applied clinical nutritionist with a private practice and consulting business in San Antonio, TX. She has been an adjunct professor and a TEDx presenter, and proudly identifies as a woman of color and uppity intersectional feminist. She is the author of dozens of books.

MORE BY DR. FAITH

Books

The Autism Partner Handbook (with Joe Biel and Elly Blue)

The Autism Relationships Handbook (with Joe Biel)

Befriend Your Brain

Coping Skills

How to Be Accountable (with Joe Biel)

This Is Your Brain on Depression

Unfuck Your Addiction

Unfuck Your Adulting

Unfuck Your Anger

Unfuck Your Anxiety

Unfuck Your Blow Jobs

Unfuck Your Body

Unfuck Your Boundaries

Unfuck Your Brain

Unfuck Your Cunnilingus

Unfuck Your Friendships

Unfuck Your Grief

Unfuck Your Intimacy

Unfuck Your Worth

Unfuck Your Writing (with Joe Biel)

Woke Parenting (with Bonnie Scott)

Workbooks

Achieve Your Goals

The Autism Relationships Workbook (with Joe Biel)

How to Be Accountable Workbook (with Joe Biel)

Unfuck Your Anger Workbook

Unfuck Your Anxiety Workbook

Unfuck Your Body Workbook

Unfuck Your Boundaries Workbook

Unfuck Your Intimacy Workbook

Unfuck Your Worth Workbook

Unfuck Your Year

Zines

The Autism Handbook (with Joe Biel)

BDSM FAQ

Dating

Defriending

Detox Your Masculinity (with Aaron Sapp)

Emotional Freedom Technique

Getting Over It

How to Find a Therapist

How to Say No

Indigenous Noms

Relationshipping

The Revolution Won't Forget the Holidays

Self-Compassion

Sex Tools

Sexing Yourself

STI FAQ (with Aaron Sapp)

Surviving

This Is Your Brain on Addiction

This Is Your Brain on Grief

This Is Your Brain on PTSD

Unfuck Your Consent

Unfuck Your Forgiveness

Unfuck Your Mental Health Paradigm

Unfuck Your Sleep

Unfuck Your Work

Vision Boarding

Woke Parenting #1–6 (with Bonnie Scott)

Other

Boundaries Conversation Deck

How Do You Feel Today? (poster)

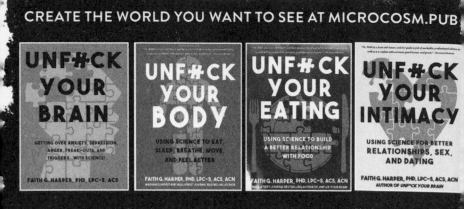